Hundred Years' War 1337–60

# Longbowman
## VERSUS
# Crossbowman

David Campbell

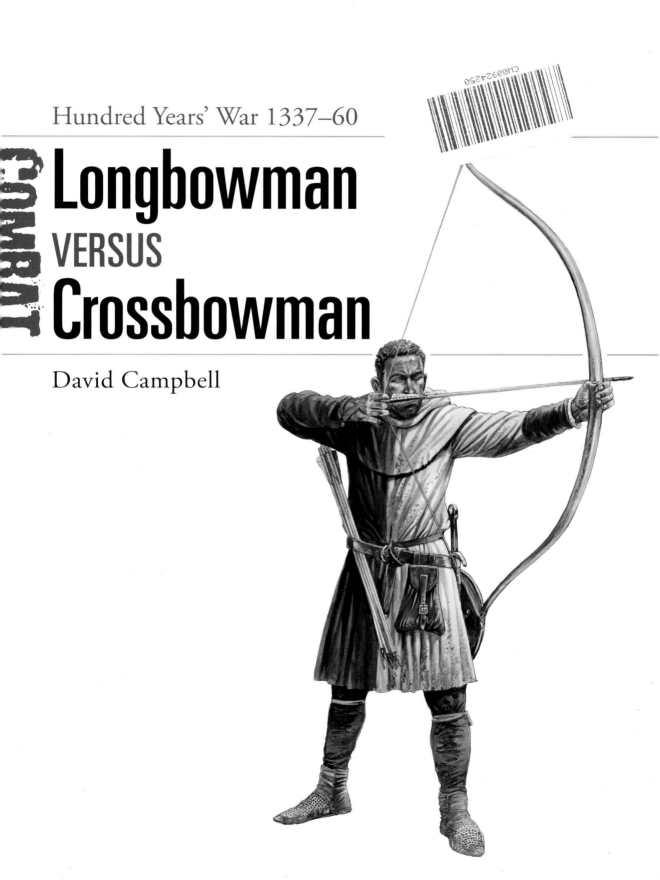

First published in Great Britain in 2017 by Osprey Publishing,
PO Box 883, Oxford, OX1 9PL, UK
1385 Broadway, 5th Floor, New York, NY 10018, USA
E-mail: info@ospreypublishing.com

Osprey Publishing, part of Bloomsbury Publishing Plc

OSPREY is a trademark of Osprey Publishing, a division of Bloomsbury
Publishing Plc.

A CIP catalogue record for this book is available from the British Library.

Print ISBN: 978 1 4728 1761 7
PDF e-book ISBN: 978 1 4728 1762 4
ePub e-book ISBN: 978 1 4728 1763 1
XML ISBN: 978 1 4728 2327 4

Index by Rob Munro
Typeset in Univers, Sabon and Adobe Garamond Pro
Maps by bounford.com
Originated by PDQ Media, Bungay, UK
Printed in China through World Print Ltd.

17 18 19 20 21   10 9 8 7 6 5 4 3 2 1

Osprey Publishing supports the Woodland Trust, the UK's leading
woodland conservation charity. Between 2014 and 2018 our donations
are being spent on their Centenary Woods project in the UK.

To find out more about our authors and books visit
www.ospreypublishing.com. Here you will find extracts, author
interviews, details of forthcoming events and the option to sign up for
our newsletter.

## Dedication

To Graham Campbell, to keep him entertained whilst he awaits his
lottery win.

## Acknowledgements

Particular thanks are due to Nick Gribit, for his generous help in making
available to me sections of his book, *Henry of Lancaster's Expedition to
Aquitaine, 1345–46*, prior to its publication, as well as for his suggestions
and advice, all of which were valuable and most gratefully received; to
Sean Andersson and Rob Kinsey of Boydell & Brewer for their assistance
in contacting Nick Gribit; to Tod Todeschini of www.todsstuff.co.uk
for his kind permission to use images of his hand-made reproduction
crossbows, as well as his advice and introduction to other experts within
the longbow and crossbow community; to Ludovic Bonneaud for his
kind permission to reproduce his photograph of the battlefield of Poitiers;
to Glennan Carnie for sharing his expertise on the longbow of the 14th
century; to the staff of Southsea Library for putting up with my inter-
library loan fetish; to Geoff Banks for midnight tea runs and the surreal
discussions over his proposed mannequin-rental empire that accompanied
them; and to Nick Reynolds, who does most of the heavy lifting.

## Artist's note

Readers may care to note that the original paintings from which the
battlescenes in this book were prepared are available for private sale. All
reproduction copyright whatsoever is retained by the Publishers. All
enquiries should be addressed to:

Peter Dennis, 'Fieldhead', The Park, Mansfield, Nottinghamshire
NG18 2AT, UK, or email magie.h@ntlworld.com

The Publishers regret that they can enter into no correspondence upon
this matter.

## Editor's note

In this book measurements are given in metric units of measurement, with
imperial equivalents given depending on the context. The following data
will help when converting between imperial and metric measurements:

| | | |
|---|---|---|
| 1 mile = 1.61km | 1yd = 91.44cm | 1kg = 2.20lb |
| 1km = 0.62 miles | 1ft = 30.48cm | 1lb = 0.45kg |
| 1m = 1.09yd | 1in = 2.54cm | 1oz = 28.35g |
| 1m = 3.28ft | 1cm = 0.39in | |
| 1m = 39.37in | 1mm = 0.04in | |

# CONTENTS

# Introduction

There were many causes, some proximate and others long-standing, that drew the kings of England and France into war with one another in 1337, but the generational dynastic wrangling over the province of Aquitaine in south-west France was the most important. The Plantagenets had ruled in Aquitaine since 1152, and it would not be wrong to assume that they thought of such a province much as they would any other under their power:

> The kings of England were the immediate and 'natural' lords of the area, and a certain long-standing loyalty to them was evident at every stage of the war. Of course it was cut across and undermined by other interests and by rival claimants to the fidelity of the Gascons, but that was a commonplace of most so-called princely states of later medieval France. (Vale 1994: 69)

By the middle of the 13th century, English fiefdoms in France (present in some form since 1066) were on the wane across the country. The Treaty of Paris,

An image of John Lackland, one of England's more dismal kings, in battle with Philippe II Augustus of France at Bouvines, 1214. John's defeat at this battle was significant, domestically and internationally; for the French it signalled the rise of a central monarchy as well as the ascendancy of French arms that was to dominate Europe for over a century, but for the English it heralded the final loss of Normandy and the effective collapse of the Angevin Empire (not to mention domestic strife that resulted in Magna Carta). The retention of Aquitaine would cause problems long after the Treaty of Paris supposedly resolved the issue in 1259. (© The British Library Board, Royal 16 G VI f. 376v)

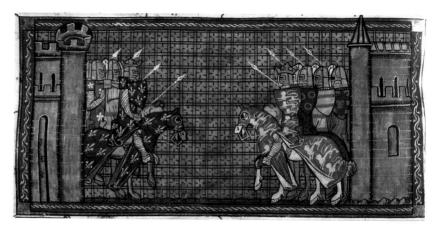

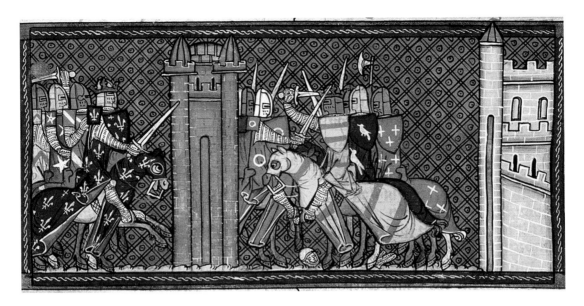

signed in December 1259, was meant to settle the dispute over the King of England's French possessions, acknowledging the permanent loss of Normandy and associated lands but retaining the Duchy of Aquitaine. In so doing, the King of England became a vassal of his French counterpart, a vassal who had to pay public homage to his lord on the occasion of succession in either the French or English royal lines. Such obeisance stuck like a bone in the throat of more than one English king, and, when coupled with the French crown's more or less regular violations of the English king's rights in his duchy (some well-deserved, some not), Aquitaine became a diplomatic open wound, infecting all other aspects of Anglo-French relations.

For the English this was compounded by the issue of Scotland. Edward I's wars against the Scots had resulted in a Franco-Scottish pact, originating in 1295 and cemented anew in 1326, to aid one another in wars against their mutual neighbour. Such a constant threat on England's exposed northern border was justifiably intolerable for Edward II and Edward III, both of whom prosecuted a series of wars against the Scots in part because of the danger the Franco-Scottish alliance posed to English security. Aside from the boiling mistrust it fomented, the alliance played a material part in the gradual move towards war when Philippe VI chained the resolution of English demands in Gascony to the political desires of his ally the Scottish king, a policy that 'was tantamount to not only preventing any advance in negotiations over outstanding problems in Gascony, but also to preventing a settlement over Scotland' (Curry 2002: 23). For Edward III the alliance between France and Scotland was poisonous, and he aimed for his subjects to see it in the same way: 'Englishmen were persuadable. They lived in a relatively small, cohesive country and were susceptible to propaganda and shared emotions that would quickly have faded in the disparate vastness of France. Philip VI had come to seem to many Englishmen the main barrier to the successful occupation of Scotland, and Scotland was a real threat, profoundly hated' (Sumption 1990: 180).

Provocation led to retaliation, which escalated into raids and attacks along the Channel coast and throughout Aquitaine, creating a Gordian knot of

An image of knights fighting in Aquitaine. Ever since the Treaty of Paris in 1259 the province of Aquitaine had proved to be a more or less constant problem, as often the cause of trouble as it was the ideal location for proxy fights between the English and French crowns. The province was a mish-mash of fiefdoms with a dizzying array of feudal obligations that were complicated by the more practical and venal aspects of medieval power politics. The English king, so far away from his troublesome possessions, was always at a disadvantage compared with his French cousin. (© The British Library Board, Royal 16 G VI f. 367)

Though France was undergoing a drawn-out period of social and political change during the first half of the 14th century, it still 'consisted of a Royal domain, five great Duchies, 47 Counties, several dozen Viscounties, and numerous other fiefs with differing titles' (Nicolle 2000: 4). The most troublesome were Brittany, Flanders and Aquitaine, provinces where the sense of independence was strong (for good historical reasons) and attachment to the French monarchy very weak, and where as a result encroachments by the French crown were particularly unwelcome. Of the three it was the quarrel over Aquitaine, the personal duchy of the King of England, that would be the catalyst for war. The rights by which the far-distant English king commanded his province had eroded over time, historian Geoffrey Templeman contending that 'such rights had become in fact what they had always threatened to become: nothing more than elaborate property rights regulated by feudal conventions' (Rogers 1999: 238). Such a transformation threatened to turn Edward III into the King of France's tenant, a direct challenge to his authority and status.

The Duchy of Aquitaine itself had once been a much more substantive holding, but the endless disagreements with the various kings of France (not to mention some of the duke's own vassals in Gascony) had led to a series of gradual – and occasionally not so gradual – encroachments that, by the time the war started in earnest, left Aquitaine something of a gnawed rump. The power of the local lords was sustained by the English crown in part through the provision of supplies and troops to help garrison the numerous castles that dotted the landscape and which were the key to its defence; however, the exigencies of fighting wars in Scotland coupled with the sheer difficulty engendered by the communications and logistics of the age meant that oftentimes the duke's vassals had to shift for themselves.

Both Brittany and Flanders had strong political and economic links to England, and together with Aquitaine it was these 'three principalities of the Atlantic coast … [that became] parties to a French civil war in which ancient territories sought to challenge the imposing constitutional edifice which the French kings had begun to erect in the twelfth and thirteenth centuries' (Sumption 1990: 37).

problems that the diplomatic structures of the time were unable to resolve. Philippe VI, not minded to indulge the English any longer, refused to treat with Edward, deciding instead to seize Aquitaine whole, setting the stage for war by issuing the *arrière-ban* at the end of April 1337. Edward's response, issued in a manifesto that August, put his case succinctly, observing that the King of France was

> striving by all means that he could to undo the King of England and his people, so that he could keep what he had wrongfully withheld and conquer more from him, refused all offers, but, seeking his opportunities, busied himself in aid and maintenance of the Scots, the enemies of the King of England, attempting to delay him by the Scottish war so that he would have no power to pursue his rights elsewhere. (Quoted in Curry 2002: 29)

War was inevitable, though the form it took and how it was fought would come as a rude shock to France.

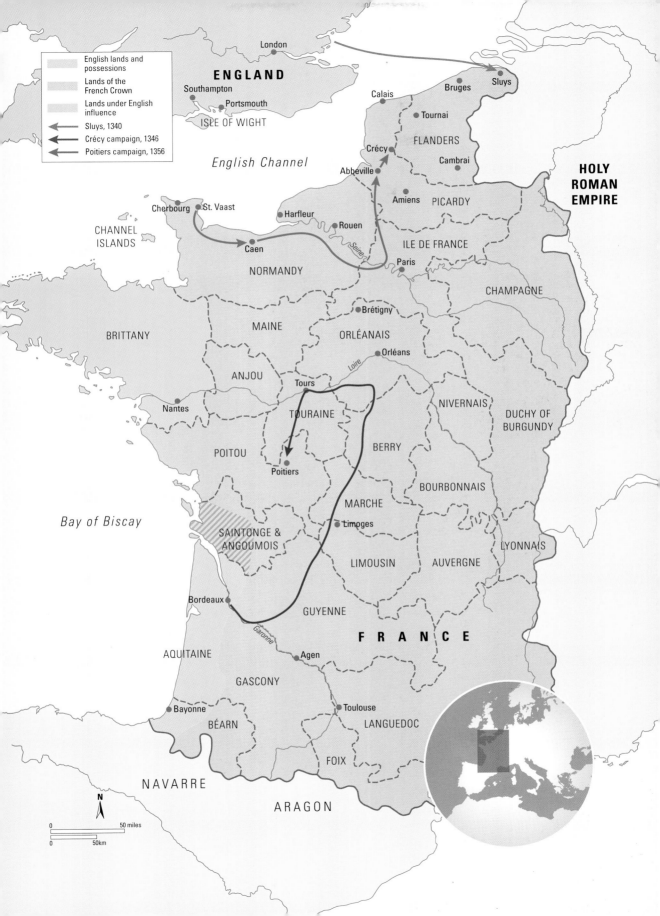

LONDON

ENGLAND

Southampton
Portsmouth

ISLE OF WIGHT

English Channel

CHANNEL ISLANDS

Cherbourg • St. Vaast

Caen

NORMANDY

Harfleur

Rouen

Seine

Calais

Bruges

Sluys

Tournai

FLANDERS

Crécy

Cambrai

Abbeville

Amiens

PICARDY

ILE DE FRANCE

Paris

HOLY ROMAN EMPIRE

CHAMPAGNE

Bay of Biscay

BRITTANY

Nantes

MAINE

Brétigny

ORLÉANAIS

Orléans

Loire

ANJOU

Tours

TOURAINE

POITOU

Poitiers

BERRY

NIVERNAIS

DUCHY OF BURGUNDY

BOURBONNAIS

MARCHE

Limoges

LIMOUSIN

AUVERGNE

LYONNAIS

SAINTONGE & ANGOUMOIS

Bordeaux

GUYENNE

F R A N C E

Garonne

AQUITAINE

Agen

GASCONY

Bayonne

Toulouse

LANGUEDOC

BÉARN

FOIX

NAVARRE

ARAGON

- English lands and possessions
- Lands of the French Crown
- Lands under English influence
→ Sluys, 1340
→ Crécy campaign, 1346
→ Poitiers campaign, 1356

N

0        50 miles
0      50km

# The Opposing Sides

## ORIGINS, RECRUITMENT AND MOTIVATION

### English

The 14th century saw a slow evolution in the way armies were raised and paid, gradually migrating away from the feudal model of obligation to one's liege towards a more systematic approach based on payment for service. There is good evidence that such feudal waters had always been rather muddier than the chivalric ethos would have liked, but the onset of the English wars in France would necessitate a more consistent and practical approach to the raising, equipping and maintaining of armies. The feudal social structure, though more or less defunct by the time of the wars with France, would still provide some of the social structure within which most recruitment would be conducted, but it became accepted practice to pay one's retinue, as well as to secure by contract any extra men that were needed for the campaign.

Though the 14th century would see a gradual evolution in English recruitment methods, in the 1340s the traditional obligations of landholders were still significant. A man with an income of £40 or more a year would often be of the knightly class, those with £25 per annum would either be a man-at-arms or would be expected to supply such a man, those with £10 a hobelar, and those with £5 – the nascent yeoman class – a mounted archer (Ayton 2011: 40–43). Mounted archers have been described by the historian Maurice Keen as 'minor landholders, not gentry, but a cut above the ordinary peasant husbandman' (quoted in Ayton 2011: 40), and were symptomatic of the evolving social flexibility that would become an increasing feature of English armies as the century progressed. (© The British Library Board, Royal 2 B VII f. 151v)

Recruitment was usually driven in the first instance by Commissions of Array (a county-based system that recruited and prepared quotas of suitable men between the ages of 16 and 60, which was in decline at this time) and by indentures to the great captains, an indenture being an agreement that such a captain 'would provide a given number of soldiers of specified types as his retinue' (Wadge 2013: 37). In addition to their immediate household they would draw to themselves friends and vassals of long standing, as well as bannerets who would come with their own retinues of men-at-arms and archers. At each level of recruitment existing ties of comradeship were crucial, from the lord to his bannerets, and from those bannerets down to 'sub-retinues and smaller companies ... [that were] often no more than a handful of men bound by ties rooted in kinship, neighbourhood or shared service [who] were the building blocks of Edwardian armies' (Ayton 2011: 21).

Those who made up the army's retinues were often experienced and used to serving together. The historian Andrew Ayton, in examining the men-at-arms of the Earl of Warwick's retinue (marshal of the army in the Crécy campaign), observes that 'all three of his bannerets and over half his knights had been campaigning since at least the mid 1330s, in most cases with some regularity ... Warwick's men-at-arms were also well acquainted with campaigning conditions in France. All except two of his knights had fought there before, the majority on at least two or three occasions' (Ayton 2011: 15).

It is reasonable to assume that a similar level of experience developed within the bodies of archers that were an ever more significant element of English armies of the period. As with the men-at-arms, for the archers (both foot and mounted) the gradual professionalization of the recruitment process as well as (arguably) the practice of warfare led to opportunities beyond those of booty; the need for well-trained and experienced men allowed social advancement (likely given a boost by the Black Death's thinning of society's ranks from 1348 onward) as well as better and more consistent payment for service. A career of professional soldiering, particularly for those who had served consistently in retinues, became an attractive prospect for more than a few men-at-arms and bowmen. The chronicler Sir Thomas Gray noted with more than a hint of disapproval how the 'young fellows who had hitherto been but of small account ... became exceedingly rich and skilful in this [kind of] war ... many of them beginning as archers and then becoming knights, some captains' (quoted in Ayton 1994: 33).

## French

The statement by historian Kelly DeVries that 'Good soldiers were always needed to fill the ranks of medieval armies, and they were always paid, whether by subsistence, wages, booty, rank, status, or nobility' (DeVries 2008: 56) was certainly true of the French army, which was composed of the feudally obliged, contracted contingents and mercenaries. The King of France had a large, powerful and rich domain at his command, though some of the advantages that such a bounteous realm bestowed were blunted to a degree by the organizational failings not

An archer (above) and crossbowman (below), as portrayed in the Luttrell Psalter (c.1320–40), one of the few contemporary sources that show bowmen and crossbowmen in England at that time. Archers were mostly drawn from rural stock, 'men who in their daily lives were accustomed to hard physical labour ... used to surviving cold, flood, disease and times of dearth ... [who] were used to violence as well as hard living and hard labour' (Strickland & Hardy 2005: 27–28). Robert Hardy notes how such men, when they had fallen foul of the law, often found a way back into society's good graces by accepting a royal pardon in exchange for service, with over 850 such occurrences being recorded for those who had served in the campaigns of 1339–40, and many hundreds more issued after Crécy and the siege of Calais. The lower detail shows a man spanning a crossbow with a belt-hook and stirrup. The process was fairly simple: with the bow reversed and pointing at the ground, the bowman would crouch and put his foot through the stirrup, and either grip the string with his hands or (for more powerful bows) snag it on a hook hanging from his belt, whereupon he would stand, the movement of his body spanning the bow. (© The British Library Board, MS 42130 f. 56r)

A goat's-foot spanning device for a crossbow, possibly Spanish, from the late 15th or early 16th century. As crossbows developed, first with wooden then composite and finally steel limbs in the latter stages of the 14th century, they became increasingly powerful and thus more difficult to draw (or span). One tool developed to make the job easier was the so-called goat's foot: a suitable bow would have a pair of lugs set in the tiller either side of the nut; the device's hooks would be attached to the bowstring, while its limbs were set against the lugs; the user then braced the tiller and drew the handle back, levering the bowstring backward until it caught on the nut. Such a device would allow the crossbowman to span bows of up to 300lb (136kg) with relative ease, and it was comparable in terms of speed with spanning using a belt-hook and stirrup. Despite the relatively high poundage of such bows, the lightness of the crossbow bolt coupled with the very short travel of the bowstring on shooting meant that the effective aimed range was perhaps 90m for most examples. They could be used to 'shower' a target in the manner of longbows, but the rapidly diminishing power of the bolt coupled with the slower rate of fire would make such an tactic much less effective. (Metropolitan Museum of Art, www.metmuseum.org)

uncommon for the time, as well as the strong regional influence enjoyed by the most powerful of the king's nobles. The traditional call to arms was made through the *arrière-ban*:

> The general *arrière ban* or summons to military service during an emergency remained, in theory and in law, though it was rarely used in practice in the decades preceding the Hundred Years' War. There would then be a remarkable revival of this tradition, which meant that despite crushing defeats at the hands of English invaders, French monarchs rarely had difficulty in raising large armies. (Nicolle 2012: 34)

Recruitment among the gentry was organized by the *Semonce des Nobles*, calling the knights of the realm to the king's banner, along with their feudal retinues; this was bolstered by the issuance of contracts (superficially similar in some ways to the English process of indenture) which drew on the large numbers of minor nobility who did not have the means to support significant households but who, like their richer and more exclusive brethren, were bred to war. Mercenary contingents, particularly those with a long-standing relationship to the French crown, were common, the ill-fated Genoese crossbowmen of Crécy being one such example. Levies from town militias (usually of spearmen, crossbowmen or archers) were also becoming an important means of bolstering numbers at the outset of a campaign, and would probably be the source of most of a French army's foot troops. David Nicolle notes that

> In wartime, local urban militias were placed under the command of captains selected by the crown in northern France, or by local barons in the south. Such captains were normally outsiders, free from local interests. Otherwise the militias were commanded by the town consul or by a captain selected from among the prominent citizens. During the second half of the 14th century many such militias were further strengthened with professional sergeants. (Nicolle 2012: 22)

As might be expected of such a cosmopolitan force the motivations of service were varied, though most could be induced by some form of booty, be it picking the pockets of the dead or – further up the social ladder – seizing an English knight for ransom. Pay, at least in the earlier phases of the war, was good, allowing for regular recruitment; but as the decades passed money became tighter, the prospects of booty less obvious, and the dangers – after so many defeats at the hands of the English – more apparent. Finally, despite the gradual shift away from Summons towards contracts, the ties of feudal obligation were still strong, both between the king and his great captains, and within the retinues of the knightly class.

# MORALE AND LOGISTICS

## English

Morale, at least at the outset of most English campaigns of the period, was good, presumably in part because of the high level of organization that Edward III's endeavours enjoyed. Aside from the sense of loyalty and the bonds of kinship that held many of the retinues together, the high prestige of the king and the reputations of his war captains played a strong role in the men's resolve to enter into campaigns willingly. Added to this was a more practical undercurrent, noted by the chronicler Jean Froissart about a later stage in the war, but still likely a factor in the 1340s and 1350s, whereby 'the less well off knights, esquires and archers of England, who appreciated [war's] comforts and, indeed, maintained their status through war' (quoted in Wadge 2013: 70).

The English expeditionary armies that harried France over the early period of the war were well supplied and equipped by a logistical system that was, of necessity, well ordered and experienced, having been refined during Edward's Scottish campaigns throughout the 1330s. One of the most important considerations was for the army to be able to sustain itself in the field for the duration of a campaign (often assumed to be around two months). The English attacks were usually launched in early summer, before the year's wheat crop would be ready for harvest, so foraging would have been a precarious proposition. English armies of the time made the most of supplies that could be seized from captured towns and villages, but such largesse, though actively sought, could not be relied upon, so a well-stocked baggage train of carts and wagons accompanied the army, ensuring that English troops could sustain the pace of their mobile operations against the French.

The purpose behind the raids and *chevauchées* was to harry the land as well as the people who worked and lived upon it; eyewitness accounts of the devastation of such practices are easy to find, as are accounts of massacres of townsfolk in the wake of sieges or battles. Despite the edicts of chivalry ordinary people often seem to have been classed in the same fashion as an enemy lord's property and chattels – fair game. The more notable massacres, however, such as that perpetrated by the Black Prince at Limoges in 1370, did not pass without comment, the chronicler Jean Froissart lamenting that 'there was no heart so hard, who had faith in God, who did not weep bitterly at the terrible mischief thus perpetrated, for more than three thousand persons, men, women and children, were killed and executed on that day' (quoted in Allmand 1973: 133). (© The British Library Board, Royal 20 C VII f. 212)

# COMBAT | Longbowman

This English longbowman has been working hard all afternoon, loosing arcing volleys of shafts into the massed ranks of first crossbowmen then score upon score of mounted men-at-arms. He is dressed in the green-and-white livery of archers raised in Cheshire and Flint, and carries only a small buckler for defence, eschewing the bulk (and cost) of a padded jacket or a haubergeon. He stands with his bow at full draw, ready to release an arrow tipped with a short bodkin point in a carefully aimed shot at an oncoming French man-at-arms. Unlike the increasingly common mounted archers, he has spent the whole of the campaign on foot, marching with his king in pursuit of an elusive French foe – until now.

## Weapons, dress and equipment

The archer was defined by his weapon, the longbow (**1**); the length and draw weight of bows varied according to the vagaries of supply and the preferences of individual archers, this example being 6ft 2in (188cm) long with a draw weight of around 140lb (64kg). He carries a ready supply of arrows (**2**) around 31–32in (78–81cm) long shoved through his belt, all short bodkin points as he expects to make aimed shots at quickly advancing armoured men less than 100m away. He wears a plain sword that is rather out of fashion (**3**), as well as a simple buckler (**4**) tied to his belt by a length of string, and a pouch (**5**) for personal items and sundries such as spare bowstrings. He wears a bracer (**6**) on his left forearm and a shooting glove (**7**) on his right hand, items that were common enough but hardly ubiquitous, depending as they did on the personal preference of the archer. His clothing consists of a liveried tunic (**8**) with a hood (the long trail of which is called a liripipe) that is cut rather longer than the most up-to-date fashion and a pair of simple hose and ankle boots (**9**), the hose tied at the knee with home-made garters. The weight of his weapons and equipment comes to around 3.5–4.5kg.

A bascinet, probably French in origin, *c.*1375–1425. Originally developed in Italy as a helmet for foot soldiers towards the end of the 13th century, the bascinet would become a common piece of equipment among men-at-arms and soldiers more generally on both sides. This example shows clearly how the aventail would attach to the vervelles (hollow staples) that stud the helmet's rim; the aventail would be edged in leather: that edge would be pierced by a number of holes that slipped over the vervelles, with a waxed cord then threaded through the vervelles, securing the aventail to the helmet. There is also a hinge to allow the fitting of a visor, which became a more common feature of the bascinet from the 1340s onwards. The initially rounded profile of such helmets changed over time, developing to a rear point through the second half of the 14th century. (Metropolitan Museum of Art, www.metmuseum.org)

The households of the king and his more important nobles would most likely see to their own supplies through private means, including victualling by their own ships, but such an approach would be insufficient for the bulk of any serious army. Historian Craig Lambert notes that there were three major systems Edward III had at his disposal for supplying his expeditionary forces: the issue of general purveyance orders, which 'allowed the king to order anyone to sell foodstuffs and other supplies to the royal purveyors' (Lambert 2011: 53); the ordering of county sheriffs to gather supplies from their locality which would then be forwarded on to designated collection points; and the commissioning of powerful merchants to source and supply all the food and equipment a garrison or army might need (Lambert 2011: 53–54).

An image of Parisians removing crossbows from storage. The production and storage of weapons, both on a regular basis for the equipping of garrisons and on the none-too-infrequent requirements brought about by a prospective expedition, was generally well-ordered and understood. In England in particular, where much documentary evidence for the period survives, a clear picture emerges of a central authority (the king's household) organizing the procurement and distribution of crossbows, bowstaves, bowstrings, bundles of quarrels, sheaves of arrows and the like, in anticipation of the king's needs when on campaign. (© The British Library Board, Royal 20 C VII f. 132)

# French

For the knighthood of France the prospect of war was most welcome. Perhaps more so than in any other country, the French aristocracy understood its own virtues and privileges through the prism of chivalry, within which feats of arms were the most important route to achieve and sustain personal glory. Though

Rioters pillaging a house in Paris. Theft, damage to property and the disruption of the civilian way of life was not an unfortunate by-product of medieval warfare – it was usually the point. The purpose of small raids, incursions and *chevauchées* was to wreak havoc on the land and people who lived on it, sacking towns, burning crops, carrying off booty, and generally making life intolerable for the inhabitants, wrecking the local economy while demonstrating their lord's inability to protect them. Often the damage caused was enough of a justification in itself, though with Edward III's excursions there was an underlying desire to provoke the harried King of France into giving battle, because it was in battles that the more significant issues were decided. (© The British Library Board, Royal 20 C VII f. 41v)

# COMBAT | Crossbowman

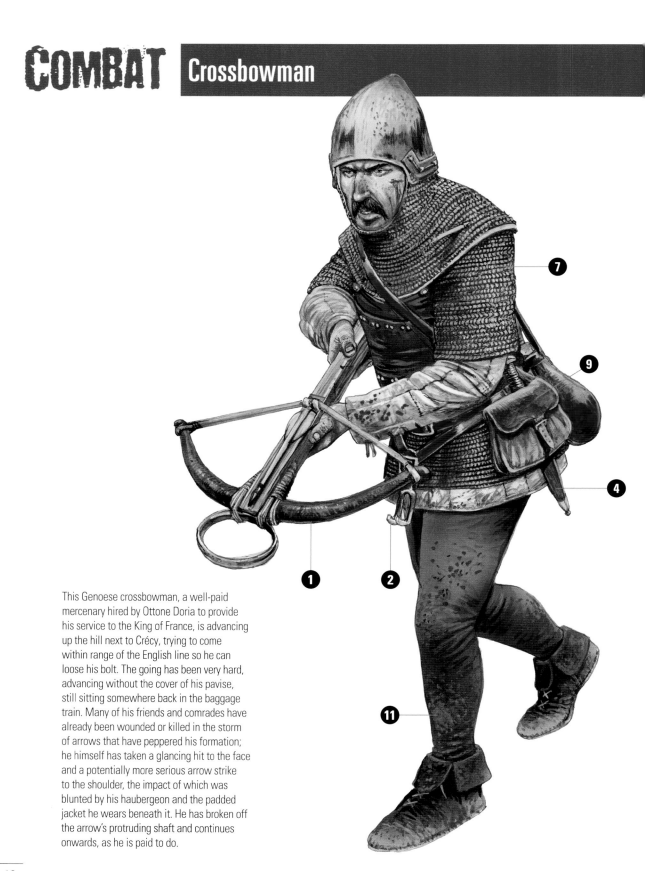

This Genoese crossbowman, a well-paid mercenary hired by Ottone Doria to provide his service to the King of France, is advancing up the hill next to Crécy, trying to come within range of the English line so he can loose his bolt. The going has been very hard, advancing without the cover of his pavise, still sitting somewhere back in the baggage train. Many of his friends and comrades have already been wounded or killed in the storm of arrows that have peppered his formation; he himself has taken a glancing hit to the face and a potentially more serious arrow strike to the shoulder, the impact of which was blunted by his haubergeon and the padded jacket he wears beneath it. He has broken off the arrow's protruding shaft and continues onwards, as he is paid to do.

## Weapons, dress and equipment

He is armed with a composite crossbow (**1**) that has a draw weight of 300lb (136kg), necessitating the use of a double-pronged spanning hook attached to his belt (**2**) in conjunction with the bow's foot stirrup to allow him to reload the weapon. The crossbows carried by Genoese mercenaries were usually composite models that were slightly more compact than those used by other troops because of their frequent employment on the decks of ships. He carries a quiver (**3**) made of wood and leather that contains a dozen bolts stored point upwards, and has a baselard dagger (**4**) for general use as well as close-quarter defence. He wears a bascinet (**5**) with aventail for protection of his head, neck and shoulders (the vervelles on the bascinet – the studs on the helmet to which the aventail is

attached – stop at the temple, showing it to be an older model, from 1350 or before). His torso is covered by a coat-of-plates (**6**), a flexible overgarment that is lined with rows of metal plates that afford the wearer both protection and more manoeuvrability than a breastplate (it was also much cheaper); underneath the coat-of-plates he wears a mail haubergeon (**7**) over a padded arming jacket (**8**) usually called an aketon or gambeson, making him very well armoured. He carries a small pouch (**9**) for personal items, a water bottle (**10**) long since emptied on his tiring march to the battlefield, and plain hose (**11**), the lack of any sort of leg armour being not uncommon for a man-at-arms or crossbowman of the time. The weight of his weapons, armour and equipment comes to around 20kg.

there wasn't an idea of national identity in the modern sense of the term, the French forces that marched against the English invaders knew they were defending their own lands and people, and this must have stiffened the sinews somewhat before an engagement. Despite this, many of the troops, especially those militia units gathered in haste, were 'Ill-trained and quickly scared on the battlefield … [and] an unreliable part of the army' (Schnerb 2005: 266).

The gradual shift towards contracts (as well as the employment of mercenary contingents that could in some cases be justifiably described as professional) led to more competent and organized units with a greater sense of their own worth than was probably the case with militia or garrison troops. Nevertheless, the latter made up a substantial part of the army's foot soldiers, and their fractious and sometimes brittle character could become problematic in times of adversity. French forces were usually regional in nature unless they were led on a national campaign by the king or a significant noble. The very size of France could prove problematic when trying to anticipate and then deal with an attacking army, especially potent and fast-moving ones such as the English expeditions of the period. David Nicolle observes that 'the pressures imposed by the Hundred Years' War led to notable devolution in the defence of the French kingdom, largely as a result of the distances involved and the inadequacy of communications' (Nicolle 2012: 23).

# TRAINING, DOCTRINE AND TACTICS

## English

From the end of the 13th century English warfare underwent an evolution quite separate from the experiences of other European realms, France

An illustration of a lady hunting with bow and blunted arrows from the 'Taymouth Hours' manuscript, composed sometime around the 1330s. Aside from confirmation that hunting with bows was not unknown as a pastime among the more courtly ladies, the image shows the huntress using a blunted pile to kill a rather passive hare; blunt piles were also used for birds, other small game and more importantly for archery practice. Work by Mark Wheatley of the English Warbow Society suggests that blunt piles performed comparably to their deadlier counterparts, but were much less costly to manufacture, safer to shoot and easier to retrieve. (© The British Library Board, Yates Thompson 13 f. 68v)

The bows used by the English throughout the period were of various sizes and draw weights, and were made from a number of different woods. It seems highly likely that most bows were easily over 100lb (45kg) in draw weight, with many as high as 150–180lb (68–82kg); such weapons could shoot arrows 175–225m, and maybe beyond 275m if using barrelled arrows (shafts that tapered towards the nock and arrowhead, designed for long-range work). Longbows recovered from the warship *Mary Rose* were in all likelihood not much different from those used at Crécy. Robert Hardy, one of the experts to examine the bows, noted that: 'It was evident that all the bows were made of fine-grained yew timber, cut radially from logs along the sapwood and heartwood boundary, which allows the highly tensile sapwood to remain on the back, or convex side, of the drawn bow, lying against its own heartwood towards the centre of the log, which forms the belly or concave side of the bow, and which is probably the timber with the best resistance to compression known to man. Yew timber, if so cut and used, offers a natural spring, and no other timber has been found to surpass its combination of tensility and strength' (Hardy 1998: 115). (© The British Library Board, Royal 14 E IV f. 23)

included. Ayton contends that the fateful encounter with the Scots at Bannockburn in 1314 was the real turning point, where 'the flower of English chivalry, fighting in the traditional fashion on war-horses, were routed by a Scottish army consisting in the main of pikemen' (Ayton 1994: 3-4). The defensively minded Scottish approach, with its echoes of Courtrai (1302), seemed to demonstrate that well-ordered foot troops on good ground were 'unable to be penetrated and thus presented an impediment to victory that the English cavalry, no matter how well-armed, how noble, or how large' (DeVries 1996: 84) simply could not defeat.

Over the succeeding years English knights and men-at-arms began to fight dismounted more often, replacing the indifferent levies of spearmen that were a staple of Edward I's wars with a much more capable, better-armed and armoured foot soldier. By the Weardale campaign of 1327 all those summoned to war, both lords and the more humble, were expected to fight on foot.

Such men stood shoulder to shoulder with increasing numbers of longbowmen who were replacing the archers and crossbowmen of the earlier age. The defensive tactics of the Welsh and the Scots that thwarted the power of the horseman alone perhaps required the English to increase the number and calibre of their archers to provide the support that would allow the cavalry to play their traditional offensive role. Historian Jim Bradbury is most likely correct in his contention that it was the increase in the number of archers employed, rather than the nature of the weapon itself, that made the difference. With larger contingents of bowmen

It was possible to use mass archery and to place large groups of archers together in positions of tactical importance. When placed in good positions, and shooting in mass, the effect of archery made itself felt, and commanders increasingly recognised its value. This development can be seen through the century before the Hundred Years' War, and not least during the later stages of the Scottish War. (Bradbury 1997: 88)

Men-at-arms and archers at work. The rise of the mixed retinue – where captains would recruit mounted archers as well as men-at-arms – was one of the most important developments in the English armies of the time. (© The British Library Board, Yates Thompson 35 f. 62)

English tactics, developed in the Scottish wars throughout the 1320s and 1330s, were fairly consistent by the time of the war with France. It was common practice to form up foot troops (mostly dismounted men-at-arms) in divisions (**A**), probably three ranks deep, one behind the other offering defence in depth (Rogers 2000: 267). Cavalry (**B**), if present, would be on the rear wings or with the baggage (**C**), which would be laagered in as safe a place as could be found behind the army. The archers (**D**) would be formed on the front wings of the lead division, canted forward to allow them to enfilade enemy horse or foot who approached the main line of men-at-arms. Often holes would also be dug along the line to disrupt cavalry; it is also likely that a skirmish line of archers screened the front of the lead division, with smaller contingents detailed to guard the baggage. Crécy (1346) shows how effective archers could be in a purely defensive posture, but Poitiers (1356) demonstrates their flexibility in both defence and attack. The exact nature of how archers were deployed will probably remain contentious, but a detailed examination of the arguments (including chronicler Jean Froissart's ill-defined *herce*) can be found in Bradbury's *The Medieval Archer* (1997: 95–108).

Longbows were not a new innovation of the age – indeed it is very difficult to try to determine the exact pattern of development or evolution of the weapon, as both written and archaeological evidence is so scarce. Nevertheless, there was a definite shift in their employment within English armies, with Dupplin Moor (1332) being the first instance of battles of dismounted men-at-arms defensively arrayed with contingents of longbowmen on their flanks. Though the archers were likely not the decisive factor of the battle, the potency of their contribution was noted in the *Lanercost Chronicle*, which observed how 'the Scots were chiefly defeated by the English archers, who so blinded and wounded the faces of the first Division of the Scots by an incessant discharge of arrows that they could not support each other' (quoted in Strickland & Hardy 2005: 183). A similarly grim fate awaited the Scottish army at Halidon Hill a year later, with

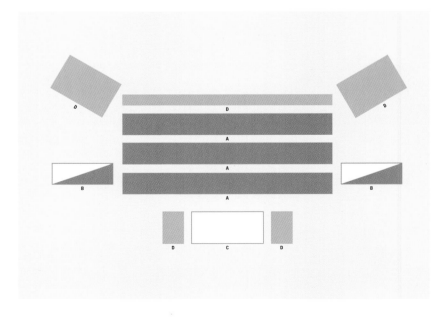

the chroniclers again noting the great damage inflicted by the English bowmen. Both battles were deliberately defensive in nature, with strong formations of dismounted men-at-arms flanked by archers who caused significant disruption to the attacking force – a pattern that would be oft repeated in France.

The role of mounted archers also became more important. Though mounting archers so that they could accompany knights and men-at-arms wasn't new, the significant increase in their numbers was. Thus the *chevauchées* (mounted raids, sometimes of significant size, that would rampage through swathes of the enemy's lands) launched by the English during this period exhibited greater manoeuvrability and offensive capability, so that 'If brought to battle, an English army consisting of balanced numbers of men-at-arms and archers could offer an effective and flexible tactical response' (Ayton 1994: 34).

As was usual with medieval armies, the men who comprised them would be expected to know their military business prior to mustering. For the knightly class this was their daily bread, but gradual changes in patterns of recruitment coupled with the crown's consistent need of armed and capable men led to an increase in the numbers of those below knightly rank who could be persuaded to follow a career in arms; such men would take care to equip themselves as well as they could afford and to master the tools of their trade. For the bowmen there was a tradition of archery on which to draw, stronger in some regions than others to be sure, but consistent and of long standing. Competitions were common, and archery practice wasn't just a pastime but a valuable practical skill, especially in the hunting of birds and small game. It is reasonable to assume that the occasions in the chronicles where a knight, desperate for a breath of fresh air, raises his visor only to receive an arrow in the face (as the future Henry V did in 1403) was the victim not of bad luck but an archer's skill.

## French

The cavalry charge was the defining act of a knight at war. Despite the occasional reverse, such as the massacre at Courtrai in 1302, the French military establishment was still firmly wedded to the concept of mounted knights driving all before them. Cavalry forces were organized into *batailles*

A German-made crossbow, *c*.1460. Though from a slightly later period, this is a good example of a composite crossbow, though it lacks a stirrup. During the early part of the Hundred Years' War, crossbows could come with wooden or composite (horn, wood and animal sinew) limbs; wooden limbs were far simpler and quicker to make, and much cheaper to boot, added to which composite bows, with their technology originating in the dry and dusty climes of the Crusades, were susceptible to damp weather and required a deal more care and maintenance. Despite such drawbacks composite crossbows were popular because they were often quite a bit more powerful than wooden bows, and were especially favoured by mercenary contingents like the Genoese (who had the expertise to look after them properly). (Metropolitan Museum of Art, www. metmuseum.org)

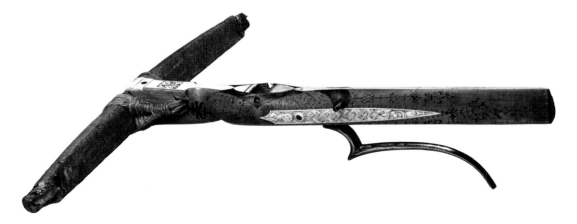

that were based on their place of origin, with the larger *batailles* being subdivided into *echelles*.

> The exact relationship between an *echelle* and a *bataille* is unclear, though the *batailles* were certainly subdivided into small *conrois* sections as they had been since Carolingian times. The *conrois* itself ... consisted of about 20–24 knights in two or three ranks, riding very close together, shoulder-to-shoulder in a manner described as *sereement*. The separate *conrois* also appear to have ridden quite close to one another. (Nicolle 2011: 44)

The basic structure and execution of such a charge had remained consistent for several centuries, in part because it worked, but also because it played into the knights' sense of their role as a battle-winning force. Most tactical deployment before and during battles was designed to produce the opportunity to launch a devastating charge, even after it became apparent that English tactics had evolved to the point where they relied upon receiving just such a charge on well-chosen ground.

When conditions were right, such as the battle of Formigny in 1450, over a century after the debacle at Crécy, a cavalry charge could still shatter an army and win a battle, but such victories were increasingly rare as the tide was turning against such tactics. Certainly there was a degree of arrogant over-confidence in the French cavalry that endured such miserable defeats at Crécy and Poitiers, driven in part by the knightly ethos of winning renown through individual feats of arms. In the fullness of time the French strategy would evolve to refuse the English the battles they desired, instead falling back on a network of strongholds and fortified towns that forced the invaders into protracted siege warfare for which they were unsuited and ill-equipped.

Foot troops, though many in number, were of variable quality and were usually deployed in *batailles* ahead of the king and the army's horse, playing a

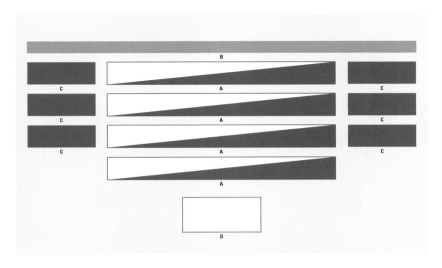

The traditional deployment for French armies, at least in some of the earlier battles of the war, was a reflection of the ubiquity of cavalry within the French military system, dominated as it was by the largest body of knights in Europe. *Batailles* of mounted men-at-arms (**A**) would line up one after another, screened by a force of crossbowmen (**B**), their flanks protected by massed foot troops (**C**), with the baggage (**D**) at the rear. Such a method of organizing one's forces can be traced back to the tactics of Crusader armies in the early 13th century where the cavalry would move forward surrounded by walls of spearmen, archers and crossbowmen, ensuring that the horsemen could retain their cohesion until the time came to charge. The initial reverses that the Valois forces suffered at the hands of the dismounted English (from Morlaix in 1342 onwards) did provoke attempts at evolution, with several instances – most notably Poitiers – of the French adopting the tactic of fighting on foot. Despite such changes they failed to achieve any commensurate increase in the percentage of crossbowmen or archers in their armies, so their formations of men-at-arms were still at the mercy of the much larger and more potent bodies of English longbowmen.

mostly passive, defensive role. This was in part due to their variable nature and reliability, drawn as they were from militias, local levies, feudal contingents, mercenary companies and contracted bodies of troops. They could certainly play a role on the battlefield, as the Genoese did at Crécy and as much of the French foot did at Poitiers, but such contributions didn't win battles, perhaps in part because they weren't expected to.

Crossbowmen were a staple of all European armies of the age, and in many ways their role hadn't much changed since the early crusades; aside from siege work and the defence of fortifications, the roles of the crossbowman in the field were to provide a protective screen behind which other troops, especially cavalry, could form up or manoeuvre, to harass and break up enemy attacks, to weaken defenders prior to a charge, and to engage with and defeat the enemy's own missile troops. The last of these roles was amply demonstrated by the French crossbowmen at Courtrai in 1302 where they met the Flemish bowmen who were protecting the main body of their army. The historian Matthew Strickland notes how 'the larger number of French crossbowmen began to tell. Their steady shooting so galled the Flemish foot that they withdrew out of bowshot, thereby yielding enough ground beyond the ditches and streams for Artois to get his cavalry across the obstacles yet still have room to reform and launch a charge' (Strickland & Hardy 2005: 135). The fact that the French charge ended in a bloody shambles should not detract from the skill and deft employment of the crossbowmen in its support.

Crossbowmen were often to be found in mercenary contingents, from places like Genoa and other cities in northern Italy as well as Provence that were well known for supplying ready-made bodies of such men. They would be well armed and equipped:

> Such troops often wore substantial body armour and normally operated in close co-operation with the *pavesari* shield or mantlet-bearers, whose role was to protect them from other archers or cavalry as they spanned and loaded their weapons. A crossbowman and a shield-bearer were in fact often paid as a team, though the man with the crossbow got more than half of the money. (Nicolle 2012: 30)

Edward III paying homage to Philippe VI. In Edward III England enjoyed a highly capable king, in sharp contrast to France. The historian Jonathan Sumption's view of the King of France's character is telling: 'Philip was an intensely serious man. What he lacked was judgement and experience. He had not been brought up to be king … although he was a competent knight and had some experience of field service, [he] was not made to be a commander of armies. He was capable of great personal courage … But he was increasingly obese and unfit, and temperamentally averse to the discomforts of campaigning and the uncertainties of the battlefield … Philip was a thoroughly bad soldier, more so than any other medieval king of France except, perhaps, for the mentally defective Charles VI' (Sumption 1990: 108). Such deficiencies of aptitude and character would cost the French dearly in the early years of the war. (© The British Library Board, Royal 20 C VII f. 72v)

# LEADERSHIP

The historian Michael Prestwich observed that:

> Successful generalship, in the middle ages as in other periods, demanded a range of qualities: strategic and tactical awareness, boldness in decision-making, persuasiveness, bravery and a measure of good fortune. The tools available to men such as Edward I or the Black Prince were limited. Communications were difficult, command structures were simple almost to a point of non-existence. Given the problems that they faced, the achievements of medieval commanders were remarkable. (Quoted in DeVries 2011: 115)

To a great degree effective leadership depended on a commander's personal reputation, his personal martial prowess, and the bonds of friendship that tied his bannerets to him.

In an age in which the monarch's rule was direct and God-given, the character and ability of a medieval king had a direct impact on all aspects of campaigning. While the English, in Edward III and later his son the 'Black Prince' of Wales, fought under warlike paragons of chivalry celebrated by more than the usual sycophants for their personal skills and abilities, the French laboured under the leadership of Philippe VI and his son Jean II. Philippe, a man who never expected to be king, was ill-fitted both physically and temperamentally for the role of monarch at war. The sons seemed to inherit the mantles of their fathers, for where the Black Prince was a naturally charismatic and talented warlord Jean II proved to be a hasty and hapless man whose personal bravery could not outweigh his military failings.

For Edward a significant part of his success as a commander was as a result of his selection of experienced and loyal 'officers' to lead battles or give support where needed (like the young Prince of Wales's array at Crécy); tried and tested men like Sir John Chandos and the earls of Warwick, Oxford, Northampton and Arundel. Edward's son had many of those same men at his side for Poitiers, where the depth of their experience compared favourably with the callowness of much of the commanding

French nobility such as Charles, the young Dauphin, just 18 years old at the time of the encounter.

The Constable was the senior military figure in France, and was responsible with the marshals for receiving, organizing and leading the army on campaign, while the master of crossbowmen, despite his title, was *de facto* in charge of all the army's foot troops. Ultimate command lay with the king, and when battle was to be joined the leadership of the army's *batailles* was taken by prominent nobles whose commands owed much to the demands of dynastic and regional politics. Mercenary cavalry would fall under the command of French knights, whereas mercenary foot contingents would be led by their own commanders, for example the Genoese crossbowmen at Crécy, who were led by Ottone Doria.

A manuscript illustration taken from the *Chroniques de France ou de St Denis* (composed *c*.1380–1400) depicting opposing forces of men-at-arms fighting one another on foot. Note the use of hafted weapons, as well as the jupon, a shorter version of the traditional surcoat that was designed with fighting on foot in mind. (© The British Library Board, Royal 20 C VII f. 214v)

An ornamental plaque of a knight on horseback, *c.*1300. The French knightly class, numbering perhaps over 4,000 in total, were the backbone of Philippe VI and later Jean II's armies, and it was they who would pay so dearly for French impetuosity on the fields of Crécy and later Poitiers. The knights would ride knee-to-knee, spaced out in several spaced ranks, with the whole unit starting at a walk and gradually increasing to a trot and then a canter. It is unlikely that charges ever went much faster, as it is impossible to keep a coherent line at the gallop, though even at a canter the noise and sight of such an enemy bearing down upon them was more than many foot troops could endure. (Metropolitan Museum of Art, www.metmuseum.org)

## COMMAND AND CONTROL

For English and French armies, sharing as they did a great deal in outlook, equipment and culture, the methods of communication and control were more or less the same. Knights of great standing could rely to some degree on their arms to distinguish them on the field, but most troops were probably not well-versed in the heraldry of those outside their immediate retinue. Banners were used to mark the position of a lord's battle, as well as to signal tactical intentions to his followers. Banners were also rallying points for troops in the crush and confusion of an engagement, with clear examples laid out in the Rule of the Templars who spelled out a hierarchy of banners to which their knights and sergeants should return if they found themselves cut off in the fray. Banners were borne both by retinues and by the individual bannerets that they contained, allowing for local command to be exercised within the broader sweep of a battle's conduct.

Trumpets were used to alert troops to prepare for movement or action, an example of which was noted by the chronicler Jean le Bel during Edward III's 1327 Weardale campaign, where a night march was to cut off a Scottish retreat across the River Tyne: 'The instruction was given for silence in the camp "in order that the trumpets might be heard: at the first sounding of which, the horses were to be saddled and made ready, at the second, every one was to arm

themselves without delay, and at the third, to mount their horses immediately, and join their banners"' (quoted in Jones 2010: 69–70). Trumpets were also used to herald the commencement of a battle, as well as to signal an order of disengagement when in the fray. Other instruments such as drums, horns and the like certainly played their part on the medieval battlefield, though it is difficult to assign them any particular role other than that of rousing one's own troops while intimidating the enemy's. It is reasonable to suppose that at least some individual retinues would have had their own recognizable instruments, and that they may have been used by the retinue captains to exercise a degree of local control or instruction among their men.

Despite such devices it was extremely difficult for medieval commanders to manage their forces in more than broad brush strokes; the initial disposition of troops together with their instructions was of obvious importance in such circumstances, after which much was left to chance and the skill and initiative of the commander's subordinates – a risky proposition in an age of headstrong and proud men. Here the quality of the king's character, and the loyalty he commanded from those below him, was a significant factor in the cohesiveness of his army once battle was joined.

An image of Charlemagne on campaign. One of the great heroes of France, Charlemagne was also a central figure in the *chansons de geste* (more specifically the Matter of France), the tales that the knightly classes enjoyed, and which were vehicles that expressed their ideals of chivalry. Originally taking hold around the beginning of the 13th century, one should not underestimate how important such ideas were to the French ruling elite, or the direct impact they had on the conduct of war by that elite. The natural tension that existed between the requirements of high chivalry and the low realities of war was stretched to breaking point; the antics of some knights in seeking trials by combat and other overtly chivalrous acts were a deliberate attempt to celebrate and prolong a martial culture that seemed in danger of fading, but which in actuality had always been more complex than the *chansons* allowed. (© The British Library Board, Royal 16 G VI f. 174v)

# Sluys

## 24 June 1340

A sword (an Oakeshott Type XIV pattern) from c.1400. Swords had been the preserve of the knightly class, often through legal proscription, but they were coming into more general use by all manner of soldiery, both mounted and foot, throughout the 14th century, though this fine example, inscribed with a line of Latin from the *Aeneid* on its pommel ('Here, too, virtue has its due reward'), is a gentleman's weapon. This style of blade, a gentle evolution of the traditional knight's arming sword, short, broad and sharply pointed, was common for the period and was meant to be used single-handed, unlike the longswords that would become more prevalent in the late 14th and 15th centuries – a change of design reflecting improvements in armour that made carrying a shield unnecessary, allowing men-at-arms to use both hands to wield a blade. (Metropolitan Museum of Art, www. metmuseum.org)

## BACKGROUND TO BATTLE

It was a peculiarity driven by diplomacy and circumstance that the start of Edward III's war with a French king over his possession of Aquitaine in the deep south-west of France should see its opening campaigns fought in and around the Low Countries. Flanders, 'rich, populous and unstable' (Sumption 1990: 185), was a French province that had no love for France, and was persuaded into an alliance with Edward through mutual hatred of the Valois crown buttered up with English trade guarantees and impressive bribes. The benefits of such an arrangement to Edward were counterbalanced by the fact that his choice of where to launch his campaign was curtailed, compelling him to pass over Aquitaine or Normandy in favour of Flanders, where he landed in 1338 and spent the best part of two years in diplomatic wranglings and inconclusive action that ended at the battle of La Capelle in October 1339. By 1340 the Anglo-Flemish alliance was thrown onto the defensive by a French assault towards Cambrai in Hainault; the decision was taken quickly to march on the old Flemish town of Tournai, then in the possession of the King of France, in the hopes of drawing his army's venom away to the north. Edward, who had returned to England in March, made preparations to bring his army cross the Channel once more in late June 1340.

Such crossings were not without risk, for the French had an active and predatory fleet, augmented by numbers of mercenary galleys hired out of Genoa. French depredations in the Channel, begun before the 'official' start of the war in 1337, were effective and deeply troubling to the English; in 1336 they had raided Orford and the Isle of Wight, and in March 1338 a force of galleys sacked and burned Portsmouth and did much the same to Jersey on the way back to Calais. Later that same year, in September, Guernsey was seized, and on 5 October another raid was conducted on England's south coast: 'And so they landed at Southampton, and killed those they found there, and plundered, and hanged many townsmen of the better sort in their own houses, and set the whole town about with flames of fire, with the greatest cruelty. But when the men of the neighbourhood came upon them, they boarded their ships and sought the open sea' (Martin 1995: 13). As Edward opened his northern campaign in Flanders the harrying of the English coast continued throughout 1339, ranging from the Bristol Channel in the west to an attempt on the Cinque Ports in the east.

The general fear and occasional panic caused by such actions was realistic, making the threat of a possible French invasion burn vividly in the minds of many Englishmen. Retaliatory raids had caused the French some problems, notably in January 1340 when a raid on Boulogne destroyed 18 highly valuable galleys and 24 merchantmen, but control of the sea was far from a settled matter. The discovery in early June that the King of France had freshly assembled a great force of ships and men caused great shock and consternation: the 'Great Army of the Sea' had taken up position in the mouth of the Zwin estuary opposite Sluys, with the express aim of preventing Edward's army from making landfall in support of his Flemish allies, either through threat or battle. If the latter was the case, it would provide an opportunity for

Though in Edward III's reign there was no navy in the modern sense of the word, the King of England did have recourse to his own small fleet of ships, augmented in times of expedition or war by 'arrested vessels' commandeered (under contract) from ports and private ownership. There was rarely an issue raising a war fleet in such a manner as from the early 14th century the design and construction of merchant ships was very similar to that of purpose-built fighting ships – both types were of a comparable size, and had integral fighting 'castles' at the stern and the bow. The crews of arrested ships were compensated for their trouble, masters of such vessels receiving 6d per day, with ordinary sailors getting 3d. (© The British Library Board, Harley 1319 f. 18)

Equipping and supplying ships in time of war was a costly pursuit. Some vessels would be adapted to the needs of the campaign (for example, having holes cut in their sides to allow them to board and transport horses), and most would require weapons and armour; in 1339 the king's ship *Philippe*, for example, received '30 padded shirts, 21 pieces of plate armour, 30 hauberks, 38 crossbows, 40 sheaves of barbed arrows, 200 cords for the bows, 13 *balistars*, 200 quarrels and 8 banners' (Lambert 2011: 58). Significant amounts of food for both men and horses was also needed, the historian Craig Lambert observing that 'A crew of forty mariners carrying forty horses, for example, could consume 2.2 tonnes of supplies per day' (Lambert 2011: 58). (© The British Library Board, Royal 20 C VII f. 26v)

Philippe VI not only to wreck Edward's fleet but also potentially to take him prisoner or kill him – an act which would likely force the English to sue for peace.

What to do became the cause of serious disagreement between an enraged Edward and some of his advisers, but for the king the chance to do battle was not to be missed. The army that had been assembling for transport as well as the ships that were to carry them to Flanders were quickly reorganized into a battle fleet that was designed for the express purpose of fighting the French off Sluys. Aside from the chance to come to grips with his enemy, Edward had to break French naval power to allow his army to land at Flanders in immediate support of his allies there, and in the longer term it was necessary to keep the Channel open if he were to have any hope of successfully prosecuting his war in either Aquitaine or Normandy. The historian Clifford Rogers also observes that Edward was well aware of the danger posed to England by ignoring such a powerful French fleet: 'It was all too easy to imagine the two hundred ships and the twenty thousand men on them descending on Britain after the king had emptied the land of its best fighting men by leading them into France' (Rogers 2000: 191). The English fleet set sail from the Orwell estuary in Suffolk on 22 June, reaching Blankenberghe off the Flemish coast the following day. According to the *Lanercost Chronicle*,

> Arriving off the coast he was informed that the fleet of Philip de Valois, at that time occupying the realm of France, was in hostile array with a great force of

A modern reconstruction of a 14th-century cog, the *Roland von Bremen*, based on an excavation of an original wreck found in Bremen dating from 1380. Though a little after the period that saw the battle of Sluys, the design is essentially the same as that of many of the French and English ships that took part in the battle. Dominated by a single mast with a square-rigged sail, the ship weighs 90 tons, is 23.2m long with a beam of 7.8m and a draught of 1.8m. Double-crewed and with a complement of archers or men-at-arms, it could bear around 100 men into battle. (Artistdesign, CC BY-SA 3.0)

Normans and French to attack him and his people. He sent forward the Bishop of Lincoln and Sir Reginald de Cobham to Sluys to stir up the Flemings (as they themselves had proposed) to fight the King of France's fleet on the morrow. (Maxwell 1913: 321)

Edward sent Cobham along with Sir John Chandos and Sir Stephen Lambkin

to reconnoitre and see how the fleet lay, and they rode on land so close to the ships that they could well see how they were equipped; and they saw some nineteen ships of such splendour and size as they had never seen before, of which one was called the *Christopher* because of its pre-eminence. In the same way they found 200 ships-of-war drawn up close to the shore in three regular lines, with other lesser ships and barges. (Martin 1995: 29)

As for the French, Jean le Bel recorded how one of the admirals of the Grand Army of the Sea 'Sir Hugues Quiéret, informed of his approach, had assembled his whole great fleet to engage the king at sea. He was prowling the waves, stalking him, convinced that he couldn't escape, given the vast number of ships at his command' (Bryant 2015: 86).

**MAP KEY**

**1** Having waited for the tide, the English fleet approaches the French position from the west; as Edward's ships come into view between the Flemish headland and the island of Cadzand they surprise the anchored French fleet by turning seaward. The English manoeuvre is designed to provide Edward's fleet with more sea room and allow his ships to come about at a more favourable angle with the wind, which is blowing from the north-east. The French ships, assuming that the manoeuvre is the beginning of an English retreat, throw off their carefully constructed wood and chain defences and break out of their mutually supporting formation in an attempt to give a ragged pursuit.

**2** Midway through the afternoon the English ships, arrayed in three broad lines and now with the wind at their backs, close with the first line of French ships. Sir Robert Morley's ship is the first to make contact in what quickly develops into a long and vicious fight that includes Edward III's flagship, the *Thomas*, which is in the thick of the battle. English ships crowded with men-at-arms grapple towards enemy vessels

that have already been weakened by showers of arrows from supporting ships of longbowmen, with captured vessels being used as platforms from which to launch new attacks on neighbouring ships. Such aggressive English tactics combined with French disorganization leads to the capture of the whole first line.

**3** The English, using their own ships as well as many of the captured vessels of the French first line, launch rolling attacks on the French second line. Flemings, observing the battle from the shore, take to their boats and join in, assaulting the French second and third lines from the rear. The resistance of the second and third lines crumbles quickly, with large numbers of French sailors abandoning their vessels in the face of the Anglo-Fleming onslaught, with many thousands drowning and those who make it to dry land set upon by bloodthirsty locals. With the exception of Pietro Barbanero's galleys (which had slipped away before the battle) and a handful of other vessels, the entire French fleet is captured.

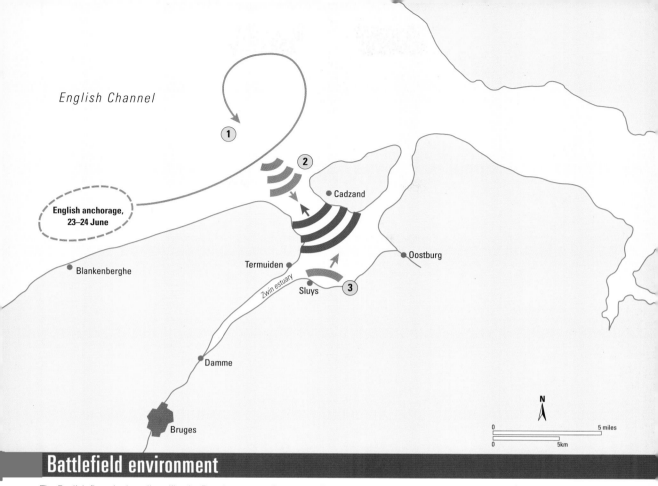

*English Channel*

① 

②

English anchorage,
23–24 June

• Cadzand

• Oostburg

• Blankenberghe

Termuiden •

*Zwin estuary*

Sluys •   ③

• Damme

Bruges

N

0                    5 miles
0            5km

## Battlefield environment

The English fleet, in three lines like the French, seems to have approached the French position from the north. The historian Jonathan Sumption gives a good description of the site of the battle, now long since silted-up and reclaimed from the sea: 'In 1340 the [Zwin] estuary was a stretch of shallow water about 3 miles [4.8km] wide at the entrance and penetrating some 10 miles [16km] inland towards the city of Bruges. It was enclosed on the north-eastern side by the low-lying island of Cadzand and on the west by a long dyke on which a huge crowd of armed

Flemings stood watching. Along the west side lay the out-harbours of Bruges: Sluys, Termuiden and Damme' (Sumption 1990: 325). The battle took place close enough to the shore to allow spectators a fine view of the proceedings, Jean le Bel recalling how Sir Hugues Quiéret, on the lookout for the English king's fleet, 'tracked him down right between Sluys and the isle of Cadzand, so that the onslaught and fighting that followed could be clearly seen from the dykes and harbour at Sluys' (Bryant 2015: 86).

**OPPOSITE** A view across the Zwin Inlet in the Netherlands. Though the actual site of the battle has long since silted up, the image gives a reasonable sense of what the shoreline was like at the time of the battle – low-lying and sandy, with scrub grass interrupted by occasional dunes. The bank in the centre of the estuary is indicative of the treacherous nature of the area, where ships always ran the risk of running aground, especially at low tide. The inclusion of John Crabbe in the king's fleet, a Flemish freebooter with much campaign experience both against and in support of the English crown, may well have been in large part due to his knowledge of such waters. (Sylfred1977, CC BY-SA 3.0)

# INTO COMBAT

The historian Craig Lambert believes that the chroniclers Adam Murimuth and Geoffrey the Baker were more or less correct in their estimations of the size of the English fleet (excluding the later Flemish contingent) comprising somewhere around 200–260 ships (Lambert 2011: 125–26). Of those ships naval historian Graham Cushway estimates that 140–200 would have been large vessels, the whole fleet 'carrying ten earls, fifty bannerets and almost 600 knights, as well as 7,000 archers and 12,000 mariners' (Cushway 2011: 93), though Rogers assumes a smaller number of ships (around 140) with commensurately fewer men-at-arms and archers (around 4,000 in total). The smaller vessels in the English fleet would have been only 30–50 tons (such vessels would normally be crewed by between eight and 15 men, though these numbers could double when putting to sea for war), while the larger ships would mostly be between 100 and 160 tons.

The French fleet that lay at anchor, chained together awaiting the English fleet, numbered 171 ships, four galleys, 25 barges and bargots (Rogers 2000: 193), the ships bearing around 20,000 sailors, with relatively small numbers of crossbowmen and only 150 men-at-arms among them. The *Grandes Chroniques de France* observed that the majority of the sailors who would be fighting against Edward's archers and men-at arms (mostly battle-hardened, one assumes, from his Scottish campaigns) were 'poor fishermen and mariners … not so skilled at arms as the English' (quoted in Rogers 2000: 196). Froissart gives a slightly different view that suggests a more robust character for the French mariners: 'And this was a very large and perilous battle because the Normans and Genoese were all proven and accustomed to the sea, and they withstood fatigue well because in all their lives they had done nothing else except pursue armed adventures on the sea' (quoted in DeVries 1995: 234). The French ships themselves were generally larger and more impressive than their English counterparts, the smallest being recorded as 80 tons, many with high gunwales and well-built forecastles and sterncastles that would make boarding them dauntingly difficult.

Though French numbers were as impressive as the size of their ships, their fleet was not as potent as it could have been. Galleys, fast and manoeuvrable vessels usually crewed by experienced mariners that would be ideal in the sort of battle that approached, were in short supply. The English raid at the start of the year that had burned 18 galleys with all their equipment at Boulogne put a serious dent in the number of such vessels available, and this served to compound the events of 1339; in a dispute over pay with Philippe VI the Genoese sailors mutinied, taking their galleys back to Italy where, thanks to bribery by ingenious English agents, they stayed. The four galleys still in French service were commanded by a piratical Genoese adventurer called Pietro Barbanero.

Though Edward was the leader of the expedition, Sir Robert Morley had the responsibility of actually commanding the English fleet (with assistance from the Flemish merchant-cum-pirate John Crabbe, who knew the waters of the Flemish coast well), especially as Edward intended to join the fight in person. Morley was a highly experienced soldier and administrator, having fought in numerous Scottish expeditions, including at Halidon Hill. In early

A representation of a sea battle off La Rochelle, with two groups of well-armed and -armoured men-at-arms. The more mundane actuality of the time was that most sea battles as well as raids on shipping, ports and coastal communities, were carried out mostly by mariners who could be English, French, Norman, Spanish, Gascon or Genoese. Such men often had some pieces of armour and would be quite well armed with bows and crossbows at their disposal. The carrying of men-at-arms was usually done once the ship had been 'arrested' and pressed into the king's service as a transport or an ad hoc man of war. (© The British Library Board, Royal 20 C VII f. 189v)

1339 he was made admiral of the northern fleet and in that role he fought a naval engagement off the Cinque Ports followed by a raid on the coast of Normandy, so he was well-versed in fighting on both land and sea. In contrast the French fleet was commanded by the admirals Hugues Quiéret and Nicholas Béhuchet, men who were neither soldiers or sailors, but rather administrators who, at least in the case of Quiéret, lacked both tactical skill and experience of war. Such drawbacks were exacerbated by the fact that they also found it difficult to work together, the *Grandes Chroniques de France* observing that 'The one could not stand the other' (quoted in Rogers 2000: 195).

On first sighting the English fleet the French commanders fell into discussion among themselves about what course of action they should take. According to the *Chronographia regum Francorum*, Barbanero

> who was in his galleys, perceiving the advent of the English, said to the admiral [Hugh Quiéret] and to Nicholas Béhuchet: 'My lords, you now see the king of England with his fleet approaching us. If you believe me, the whole fleet ought to be moved onto the open sea; for if you remain here, the English who have the wind, the sun and the flow of the water with them in so much that they will confine you because you will be able to help tour ships only minimally.' However Nicholas Béhuchet, who knew better how to make a calculation than to fight naval battles, responded to him: 'He is a coward who retreats from here and does not stand ready for the onset of battle.' (Quoted in DeVries 1995: 232)

Béhuchet's position had some validity if, as Rogers posits, he was afraid that by sailing out to meet Edward the English may have slipped past him entirely, landing unopposed (Rogers 2000: 195). Even so, Barbanero was right in his assessment of the advantages of wind and sea room that the English enjoyed, and so, Béhuchet's injunction of cowardice aside, he rowed his four galleys away, saving them while depriving the French fleet of some of its most effective warships.

For the English the appearance of the vast French fleet was equally intimidating. The *French Chronicle of London* records how 'when [the king] saw his enemies so strongly equipped, that it was a most dreadful thing to behold; for the fleet of the ships of France was so strongly bound together with massive chains, castles, bretasches [wooden breastworks], and bars' (Riley 1863: 276). Organized into three ranks, 19 of the largest and most powerful ships occupied the first line, the *Christopher* among them. (Once the pride of the English fleet, the royal ship *Christopher* had been captured with four others in a daring raid on the harbour at Arnemuiden in 1338.) The English plan was highly aggressive, consisting of a direct attack on the main French line and, through force of arms, overcoming it before moving on to the second line and so on. Froissart recounted that 'Then the king set all his ships in order, the greatest before, well furnished with archers, and ever between two ships of archers he had one ship with men of arms. Then he made another line to lie aloof with archers to comfort ever them that were most weary if need were' (Ashley 1887: 73–74). It was a novel approach, with strong echoes of the English approach to warfighting on land, except in this instance the distinctive nature of naval warfare would allow the king's men to retain the advantage of mutual support while in the attack. It is possible that some of the larger English ships could have borne both men-at-arms and archers, though it is impossible to say for certain.

Despite the size of the enemy fleet, the chronicler Henry Knighton recorded how 'King Edward seized the right moment, that Baptist's day in the morning, to take out his fleet and plough the open sea, bearing down upon the French fleet, undaunted by their arrogance and great numbers' (Martin 1995: 29). The English ships waited for the change of tide, tacking to get into a better position with the wind at their backs. The manoeuvre, so close to the French fleet, gave the appearance that the English ships were turning about and starting to flee, and caused great disruption in the carefully organized line of ships and galleys as they broke their own formations as a result, *The French Chronicle of London* describing the scene:

And then our mariners hauled their sails half-mast high, and hauled up their anchors in manner as though they intended to fly; and when the fleet of France beheld this, they loosened themselves from their heavy chains to pursue us. And forthwith our ships turned back upon them, and the melee began, to the sound of trumpets, nakers, viols, tabors, and many other kinds of minstrelsy. (Riley 1863: 276)

The English fleet, broken into three successive lines in a manner similar to that of the French, closed with the enemy vessels. The shipborne engines of war began their work, with the long iron bolts of ballistae coming from the

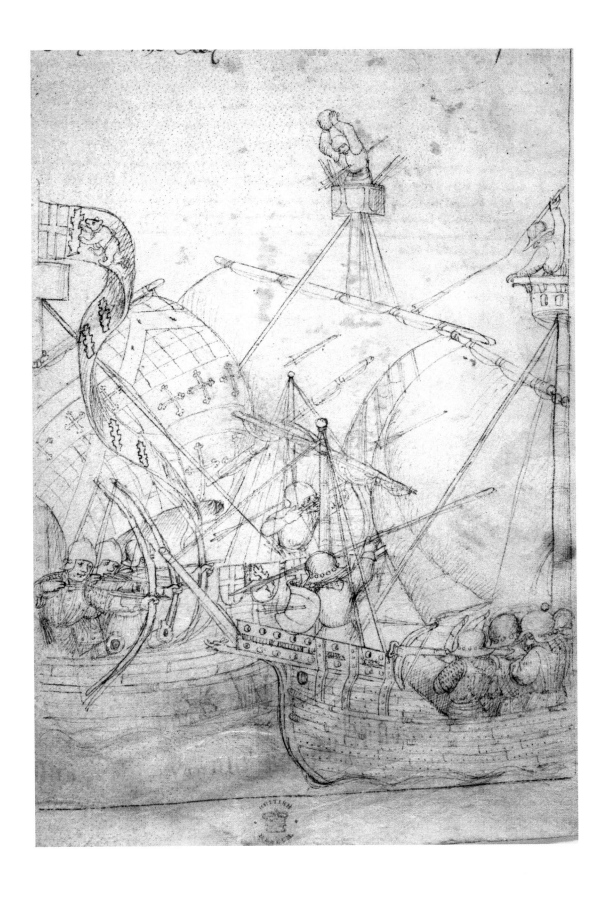

French ships matched by English springalds throwing stones and burning pitch, an overture to the arrows and bolts that soon thickened the air (Cushway 2011: 97). Morley's ship was the first to make contact with the French line, followed by others, creating a confusing and deadly melee. The dangers of such a fight were exemplified by William de la Pole's galley, that 'moving faster than the roundships, reached the French line out of range of the supporting longbowmen. Pelted with rocks by mariners on the decks above, the crew was massacred before they could even board' (Cushway 2011: 97). The dismal fate of his ship's crew exemplifies the critical importance of support by archers.

The basic English tactic, that of suppression and disruption by bowmen and to a lesser degree by crossbowmen (weapons that were common enough aboard ship and were likely used by the English sailors), thus allowing the men-at-arms to close and do their work, is described in *The French Chronicle of London*:

> Our archers and our arbalesters began to fire as densely as hail falls in winter, and our engineers hurled so steadily, that the French had not power to look or to hold up their heads. And in the meantime, while this assault lasted, our English people with a great force boarded their gallies, and fought with the French hand to hand, and threw them out of their ships and gallies. (Riley 1863: 276)

As with fighting on land, it was the combination of massed archers supporting men-at-arms that proved so effective, with the ferocious arrowstorms that English bowmen could unleash in such short periods of time killing and pinning the French crews until the swords, axes and polearms of the foot soldiers could finish the job.

The *Christopher*, symbol of lost English pride, was quickly targeted in the initial clash of vessels. Froissart described how the French

> did put their fleet in order, for they were sage and good men of war on the sea; and did set the Christopher, the which they had won the year before, to be foremost, with many trumpets and instruments, and so set on their enemies. There began a sore battle on both parts; archers and crossbows began to shoot; men of arms approached and fought hand to hand; and the better to come together they had great hooks and grappling irons to cast out of one ship into another, and so tied them fast together. There were many deeds of arms done, taking and rescuing again. And at last the great Christopher was first won by the Englishmen, and all that were within it taken or slain. (Ashley 1887: 74)

Now in English hands, the deck of the *Christopher* was quickly infested with archers, who immediately set about shooting at the men on the second rank of ships.

Edward, aboard his flagship the cog *Thomas*, was in the thick of the fighting, Froissart observing how 'The king of England was there in the flower of his youth, and he did not try to save himself, but he ventured into the battle as adventurously as any of his knights, and he demonstrated himself well in fighting with weapons if the need was shown' (quoted in DeVries 1995: 234). Such martial vigour was recorded by others, and it seems the king received a serious wound to his thigh during the battle, suggesting that the yearning for noble deeds exhibited by so many chroniclers of the time might have been justified in this particular case. Certainly Edward's reputation as a man-at-arms was never questioned by either his friends or his enemies. Geoffrey the Baker gives a visceral feel of the nature of such close-quarters fighting:

> An iron rain of bolts from crossbows and arrows from bows sent down thousands to their deaths. Those who wished or were brave enough to do so fought at close quarters with spears, axes and swords. Many had their brains knocked out by stones thrown down from the tops of masts. With no word of a lie, there was fought a sea-battle so massive and so dreadful that a faint-heart would not have dared to look upon it even from a distance. (Preest & Barber 2012: 60)

Representations of the gold noble that Edward III issued in 1344 in commemoration of his victory over the French at Sluys. The king is shown aboard his ship, the cog *Thomas* (note the forecastle and sterncastle), holding a drawn sword, symbolic of justice and his success through the force of arms, as well as bearing his quartered shield, incorporating both the English arms as well as those of France, a bold statement in support of Edward's claim to the French throne that he first made in early 1340. Such coins were important symbols of the king's power and how he wished it to be seen by both his countrymen and foreigners alike. (Private Collection / © Look and Learn / Bridgeman Images)

The type of battle where, as Thomas of Burton described it, 'the sea was colored red with blood [and] in many ships men stood with blood rising above their ankles' (quoted in DeVries 1995: 229) was exemplified by the fate of the *St James* from Dieppe, one of the greatest ships in the French line, which found itself entangled with a ship from Sandwich owned by the Prior of Christchurch; trying to tow the smaller vessel away, Geoffrey the Baker describes how the *St James* found itself in a deadly fight as the English ship's sailors 'with the help of the earl of Huntingdon put up such a stout resistance that the struggle lasted the whole night. On the next day, when the Normans were eventually defeated, the English found in the captured ship more than four hundred men slain' (Preest & Barber 2012: 61).

After some considerable period of hard fighting, the vessels in the French first line were almost all in enemy hands, Thomas of Burton noting that 'the French and the Normans were defeated by the English through fierce shooting' (quoted in Strickland & Hardy 2005: 209). Certainly the effect of English archery seems to have been ruinous on the French crews. Geoffrey the Baker commented on how the onslaught had 'driven the men from the ships' (Preest & Barber 2012: 60), acknowledging the fact that, with a battle at sea, the defeated have few places to run. Froissart's opinion was that 'This battle was right fierce and terrible, for the battles on the sea are more dangerous and fiercer than the battles by land; for on the sea there is no recoiling nor fleeing, there is no remedy but to fight and to abide fortune and every man to shew his prowess' (Ashley 1887: 75). Those not killed by archery in the approach or by the men-at-arms storming aboard would have to rely on the mercy of the attackers, which was in scant supply, or take their chances in the water.

The grim prospect that awaited the ships in the second line was all too obvious. Geoffrey the Baker noted that 'the other English ships turned their attention to dealing with the second French squadron, and with great difficulty made an assault upon it. But the men were driven out of it more easily than from the first squadron, for the French for the most part now left their ships of their own accord and drowned in the sea' (Preest & Barber 2012: 60). The attack on the second and third French lines was helped by the Flemings, many of whom had been watching the earlier stages of the battle from the shore. Taking to their boats, significant numbers of them sailed out the short distance to the rear of the French line and began setting-about their enemies with a vengeance, materially aiding the English effort. The French and Normans who abandoned their ships during this time mostly drowned,

# English men-at-arms supported by archers close with a French ship

**English view:** A moderately sized cog, freshly captured in the storming of the first line of French ships and now infested with English archers and men-at-arms, is making its way ever closer to a larger French ship in the second line. Grappling hooks have been thrown by some of the English sailors and have snagged the French vessel, drawing both ships together; there is less than 10m between the two ships, and the distance is shrinking by the moment. The air is thick with arrows but only a few of the Genoese crossbow bolts answer in return. A group of men-at-arms – a rough-and-ready bunch dressed and armed with plain purpose for the practical rigours of the encounter to come – crowd by the gunwale waiting to scramble across to the French ship when the opportunity arises. They are interspersed with archers who are shooting ceaselessly onto the deck of the French vessel to either kill the occupants or force them to keep their heads down behind their pavises. The archers all carry sheaves of arrows and knives or swords for personal protection, but for the most part they are lightly equipped, with a few wearing gambesons and cervellieres for protection, the rest in common clothes. One man-at-arms is recoiling, struck in the chest by a lucky bolt shot from one the Genoese crossbowmen, but the overall mood is one of fierce elation as they all know they are tantalizingly close to their goal.

**French view:** A French ship, defended by a contingent of Genoese crossbowmen, a few French men-at-arms and the vessel's own sailors, is under heavy attack by an English cog that is grappling its way ever closer. Nearly a score of crossbowmen, crouched behind their pavises, are putting up a valiant fight but it is a losing battle – several of them have been killed and more are wounded, all by the English arrows that splinter the deck and their shields. One of the few men-at-arms aboard has been wounded by multiple arrow strikes and leans on his polearm for support, awaiting whatever comes. The Genoese crossbowmen are professional soldiers aged from their mid-twenties up to several who could be in their early fifties, most with plenty of experience both on land and serving in the galleys of the Mediterranean Sea; their professionalism shows in their armour (most wearing gambesons and haubergeons), bascinets and weapons (powerful and accurate composite crossbows) which are well-used and well-maintained. Nevertheless, the situation is fast becoming desperate, the men harried and on the verge of panic, knowing what must come next. They are reloading their weapons feverishly, shooting whenever they can – a couple of them are daring to pop above the pavise line to loose their bolts at the English, an act that causes an English man-at-arms to crumple but which also results in one of the Genoese falling back, shot through with an arrow.

weighed down by their weapons and armour or simply because they didn't know how to swim. Those that made it to the shore found their troubles far from over as they were attacked, bludgeoned and killed by ranks of waiting bloodthirsty Flemings.

By the time the day was done the victory was undeniable. Aside from the horrendous losses of men, the French fleet had effectively ceased to exist, the vast majority of it captured, only 23 or 24 vessels of various types escaping to the open sea under cover of night (excluding Barbanero's four galleys that had left the stage earlier in the performance). Jean le Bel describes the grim reality that faced Philippe VI the next morning:

ZEESLAG VOOR SLUIS.

the French, Normans, Gascons, Bretons and Genoese were finally killed, drowned and utterly defeated: very few escaped …
Sir Hugues Quiéret and a good number of his kinsmen were killed in this battle, along with fully thirty thousand men either slain or drowned, so it was said; a great many of their bodies were washed up by the sea on the beaches of Sluys and Cadzand, some of them fully armed, just as they had fought. (Bryant 2015: 86)

Quiéret had been killed in the fight over his own ship, but Nicholas Béhuchet had survived as a prisoner, though not for long; Edward, incensed at the damage Béhuchet had inflicted on the south coast of England with his incessant raiding over the preceding years, had him hanged from his own ship's yardarm.

Losses were extremely one-sided, with the English suffering around 4,000 dead (including only four knights according to Geoffrey the Baker and Murimuth), but other chroniclers put the toll at only between 400 and 600. The assumption of the time that Philippe VI had lost 30,000 men and mariners (40,000 according to Froissart) was certainly an exaggeration, but not by as much as was usually the case with medieval battles, Cushway noting that most modern estimates assume between 16,000 and 18,000 dead (Cushway 2011: 98). Thomas of Burton, in his *Chronica monasterii de Melsa*, commented on the scale of the English victory thus:

There was such an infusion of blood that for three days after the battle in all the water of the Zwin all the way to the sea there seemed to be more blood than water. And there were so many dead and drowned French and Normans there that it was said, ridiculing them, that if God had given the fish the power of speech after they had devoured so many of the dead, they would have spoken fluent French. (Quoted in DeVries 1995: 226)

An illustration of the Flemings watching the battle of Sluys a short way out to sea, as well as the grim fate that awaited the French survivors who had managed to make it to the shore. Froissart noted how 'The news quickly spread through Flanders and Hainault and thence reached the two armies facing each other at Thun-l'Évêque. It brought joy to the Hainaulters, the Flemings and the men of Brabant, but dejection to the French' (Brereton 1978: 64). Edward III spent the following day aboard ship, receiving news from his allies, eventually disembarking and giving thanks at the church of Our Lady at Ardenburg. (© The British Library Board, The British Library Flickr Photostream)

# Crécy

## 26 August 1346

### BACKGROUND TO BATTLE

In launching his great *chevauchée* on Northern France Edward III aimed to tear great swathes of the French countryside to pieces, wrecking the local economy by hacking and burning a great arc of misery out of Philippe VI's lands, showing him to be an empty vessel unable to protect his people, and shaming him into a battle that would, hopefully, end the war in one decisive blow. As Clifford Rogers has made clear in his analysis of the Crécy campaign, Edward was explicit from the outset about his desire 'to win his rights by force of arms' (quoted in Rogers 2000: 242). The king's fleet of some 740-odd ships landed at the Norman town of Saint-Vaast-la-Hogue on 12 July 1346, and within a week of the horses being disembarked the English made their presence felt, Jean le Bel observing how 'Once they were all ashore Sir Godfrey de Harcourt, who knew Normandy and the Cotentin like the back of his hand, took five hundred men-at-arms and two thousand archers and left the king and his army and went fully six or seven leagues [*c.*29–34km] ahead, burning and destroying the land' (Bryant 2015: 171).

The royal counsellor Lord Northburgh wrote of how the king was 'boiling with eagerness to meet his enemies' (quoted in Rogers 2000: 243) as his army marched out in three divisions, Jean le Bel noting how each division would march along a separate route before converging again on a pre-arranged spot by nightfall, allowing the army to inflict the maximum amount of damage on the unfortunate lands through which it passed. The English 'were spread over a wide area even though they only had fifteen hundred mounted men-at-arms (whatever anyone else may say), and in this way they advanced, ravaging and laying waste the land for six or seven leagues on either side, burning and destroying every unfortified town and village, abbey and priory in their path' (Bryant 2015: 172).

The town of Caen, resting place of William the Conqueror, was reached on 26 July. The *Grandes Chroniques de France* records how 'when the English came before Caen, they assailed the town in four places, and shot arrows from their bows as dense as hail' (quoted in Rogers 1999: 124), storming and sacking the town but leaving the castle unmolested. The sacking of the town was soon over and in under a week it was time to move onwards, the *Grandes Chroniques de France* observing that: 'And always, Godfrey d'Harcourt, who burned and devastated the countryside, went ahead' (quoted in Rogers 1999: 124). Edward's march eastwards continued,

sacking what he could, bypassing what he could not, and reaching Fresnes on 12 August. His army tarried at Poissy, which he took on 14 August, hoping that the French would march on him and give battle. He waited in vain.

The apparent hesitancy of the French to take the English to task, especially when they were so close, was noted in the *Grandes Chroniques de France*, which observed in amazement how 'the nobles had the boats scuttled and the bridges broken everywhere the King of England passed, when they should, quite the contrary, have crossed over to him over the bridges and in the boats, for the defense of the country' (quoted in Rogers 1999: 127). The chronicler avoids blaming the French king for such a lily-livered approach, though Jean le Bel shows no such compunction: 'I just don't understand it. To put it bluntly, he never had the stomach or the courage to fight' (Bryant 2015: 175). Edward started his move north at a pace of nearly 24km a day, with Calais his likely goal. Shadowed by the now active French army, Edward knew he had to cross the Somme to guarantee himself a line of retreat, and sent scouts to find the best way over the river.

On 24 August the English army, led by a willing local guide, made their way to a ford over the Somme at Blanchetaque. Forced to wait for the tide to ebb, the English soon saw strong French forces led by Godemar du Fay begin to array themselves on the far bank, numbering 500 men-at-arms and 3,000 armed common people according to Lord Northburgh. Despite this setback the English pressed on, Jean le Bel observing that 'the French fought like fury to stop anyone reaching the further bank; the first wave had a hard time getting across, and a good few were killed and wounded in the river. Nonetheless the English made the crossing and the French were routed and put to flight, leaving a great many dead in the fields' (Bryant 2015: 178). Edward himself records that it took only an hour and a half for his whole army to cross the river.

The English fleet assembled by Edward III for what would become the Crécy campaign of 1346 was to be the largest of the century. Preparations began the summer beforehand, with the historian Craig Lambert observing that from start to finish it took over nine months to organize and assemble (Lambert 2011: 104–06). Between 80 and 90 ports supplied a total of around 720 to 747 ships crewed by approximately 15,000 mariners; they were to transport around 3,000 men-at-arms and their horses, the same number of mounted archers, and 8,000 more foot troops mostly comprised of archers, giving a total, including non-combatants, of 15,000–20,000 men and 15,000 horses (Lambert 2011: 140). Large flotillas assembled at Portsmouth and Sandwich, sailing for the French coast and landing at la Hougue on 12 July. (© The British Library Board, Royal 20 C VII f. 25v)

**MAP KEY**

**1** On the morning of 26 August, Edward III forms his army on a ridge between Crécy and Wadicourt, a strong defensive position. His three divisions of dismounted men-at-arms are organized in three lines, the first of which (the Prince of Wales's division) is flanked (and probably also screened) by bodies of archers. The baggage lies to the rear, protected by more archers. The army rests and eats, awaiting the French.

**2** At roughly 3pm Philippe VI's army comes within striking distance of the English. The French king's initial intention, to hold off the attack until the morrow, is frustrated by the knights of the leading *batailles* who refuse to back away once the English have been sighted. At about 6pm the Genoese crossbowmen, having rapidly formed up before the Comte de Alençon's *bataille*, advance on the English position without their protective pavises, which are trapped in the baggage train some way behind the main force. They are shot down by the English bowmen and are forced to retreat in disorder.

**3** The knights of the first *bataille* led by Charles II, Comte de Alençon, seeing the collapse of the Genoese crossbowmen, begin their charge before the retreating foot troops have had a chance to clear the field, riding many of them down. Ottone Doria, their commander, is also killed. Alençon's charge loses all cohesion and is brought to a bloody halt by the repeated volleys of the English archers.

**4** The second of the great attacks is launched against the Prince of Wales's division, led by the kings of Bohemia and Majorca and the Duke of Lorraine; the advance reaches the English line but is thrown back with great loss to the French, including the kings of Bohemia and Majorca and the Duke of Lorraine, all of whom are killed.

**5** With darkness approaching the final attack, supposedly led by Philippe VI himself, fails to make a dent in the English line, petering out in a series of ever weaker charges. The King of France flees the field in the company of Sir John of Hainault.

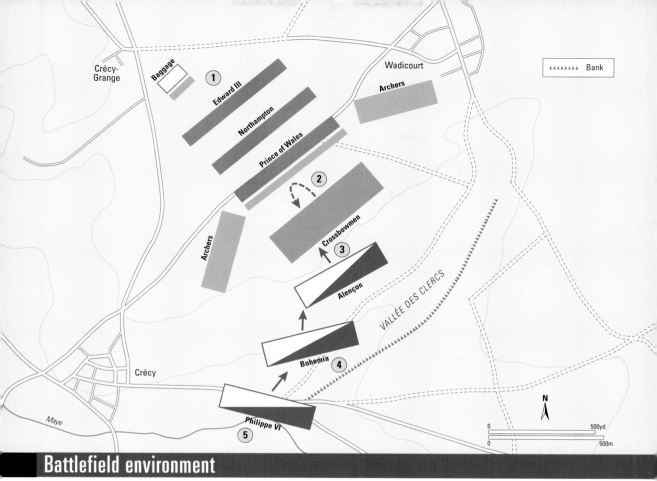

Map labels:

Crécy-Grange
Baggage
1
Edward III
Northampton
Prince of Wales
Wadicourt
Archers
2
Archers
Crossbowmen
3
Alençon
VALLÉE DES CLERCS
Bohemia
4
Crécy
Philippe VI
5
Maye
N
0 — 500yd
0 — 500m
▲▲▲▲▲▲▲▲ Bank

## Battlefield environment

Sir Philip Preston's description of the battlefield at Crécy cannot be improved upon: 'The traditional battlefield lies north-east of the village of Crécy-en-Ponthieu, and consists of the gentle western slope and flat-bottomed bed of the valley known as La Vallée des Clercs. Its length from north to south is almost two kilometres, and its width on the floor of the valley at mid-point, is about 200 metres. The width diminishes to approximately 100 metres at either end … Its western limit is a ridge (75 metres) running from Crécy at its south to Wadicourt to the north. Its northern limit (65 metres), and diametrically opposed to the traditionally accepted direction of the advancing French army, is the narrowing head of the valley beneath Wadicourt. Its southern limit (35 metres), defined to the west by the rising ground towards Crécy and the sloping side of the valley to the east, is the mouth of the valley where it sweeps down to join the valley of the River Maye. Finally, and critically, its eastern limit is the eastern side of the valley itself, a distinct topographic feature consisting of a tall, steep and almost sheer bank running the full two kilometres of the length of the valley. Generally the height of this bank is between 2.5 and 5.5 metres above the valley floor' (Preston 2005: 123). The bank on the eastern side of the valley would have denied the French army a direct line of approach to the English position, forcing them to funnel through either the narrow northern or southern entrances of the Vallée des Clercs before they could form up to attack.

**OPPOSITE** A view of the battlefield of Crécy-en-Ponthieu, on top of the ridge at the approximate location of the Black Prince's division, with Wadicourt just visible to the far left of the picture. The state of the ground is similar to how it would have been at the time of the battle, which was fought after the crops were harvested. The French approach would have been from the right, forming up in the bowl of the Vallée des Clercs and then advancing uphill. If, as some of the chroniclers reported, there had been a short but intense downpour just as the battle was starting, it would have made marching or riding over such terrain more difficult. (Paul Hermans, CC BY-SA 3.0)

# INTO COMBAT

The English, according to Froissart 'fearing nothing now that they had the river Somme behind them' (quoted in Rogers 2000: 264), moved slowly until they found good ground on which to fight; Lord Northburgh observed how:

> that night [the 24th] the king of England made camp in the forest of Crécy, next to the river, because the French army appeared on the other side after we had crossed; but [the King of France] did not wish to cross over to us, and returned towards Abbeville. And the following Friday the king of England camped once more in the forest of Crécy. And on the Saturday morning he set out towards Crécy …
> (Quoted in Ayton 2005a: 99)

Philippe tarried at Abbeville all day on 25 August, until word finally came that the English were near Crécy, whereupon he set out with his host on the morning of the 26th, marching for 21km for a chance to catch the English king.

The English army – 2,500 men-at-arms, 5,000–6,000 longbowmen, 3,000 hobelars and mounted archers, and around 2,000–3,000 spearmen – positioned itself at the top of a slope that led down into the Vallée des Clercs, anchored by Crécy on their right and Wadicourt on their left. Edward made an impromptu fortification out of his baggage train, positioned to the rear of his three divisions, the exact dispositions of which are the subject of much disagreement in the sources and among the historians that interpret them, though all agree that the divisions were commanded by King Edward, the Prince of Wales and the Earl of Northampton. As to their deployment, the Prince of Wales's division was to the front, with Northampton's and then the king's directly behind (Prestwich 2005: 143–44). Thus the first division under the Prince of Wales would receive the brunt of any attack; Geoffrey the Baker noted that 'in a short time they dug many holes in the ground in front of their first array, each hole being one foot deep and wide' (Preest & Barber 2012: 73), so as to frustrate any horsemen who advanced so far.

The positioning of the archers is also contentious, with Geoffrey the Baker offering one of the more famous descriptions:

> they stationed their archers with great care, so that they formed as it were the wings on the sides of the king's army and were not together with the men in armour. In this position they did not impede their own troops, and, instead of attacking the enemy head on, they sent the lightning flashes of their arrows into his flanks.
> (Preest & Barber 2012: 73)

Having the flanks anchored with large numbers of archers was sensible, though Robert Hardy's conjecture that there would likely have been a screen of archers ahead of the Prince of Wales's division seems reasonable, despite Geoffrey the Baker's view – archers outnumbered all other troop types in the king's army, so they must have been there to work. (Strickland & Hardy 2005: 295–97). The historian Matthew Bennett agrees that it is likely that 'the archers could have started in front of the men-at-arms before falling back to the flanks as an enemy approached' (Bennett 1994: 8–9).

As the afternoon progressed the French host was fast approaching from Abbeville. A vast army at least double the size of the English force and organized into at least four, maybe as many as nine *batailles*, the first of which was led by Charles II, Comte de Alençon, its heart consisted of around 12,000 knights and mounted men-at-arms, supported by around 4,000–6,000 crossbowmen (including the Genoese) and many thousands of foot troops made up from levies, militias and the like. The army's approach to the English position was hampered by a bank that runs along the north-eastern side of the valley which created a 'potential topographic trap. With restricted access into the valley from the east, the principal lines of attack open to the French would have been from the mouth of the valley at the south or, by means of a wider sweep, into the head of the valley from the north' (Preston 2005: 123). Thus it was that the French foot and horse had to navigate a narrow turn to get into the Vallée des Clercs, throttling the advance of the army and denying the King of France the full advantage of his considerable numbers.

Philippe, learning of the closeness of the English to his own host, asked the advice of one of the knights who had scouted the English position, and was told:

Sire, your army is trailing a long way back across the fields and it'll be very late by the time they're all assembled – it's already past none [3pm]. I suggest you order your men to make camp here; then tomorrow morning after mass draw up your battalions and attack your enemies in the name of God and Saint George, for I'm sure they won't have fled: from what I saw they'll be waiting for you. (Bryant 2015: 180)

Such counsel, however wise it may have been, could not compete with the reality that was developing on the field in front of the king.

Froissart has it that hot blood played a crucial part in the start of the battle: 'When King Philip came to the place where the English stood and saw them, his blood was up. He hated them so much that he could not renounce to fight. He said to his marshals, "Send our Genoese crossbowmen ahead and let's begin the battle, in the name of God and of my lord saint Denis!"' (quoted in Schnerb 2005: 271). The king's order for the crossbowmen to advance was more likely due to the uncontrollable fire of his subordinates rather than any wild passions of his own. Jean le Bel tells of how the king ordered all his banners to hold back, but that being within striking distance of their long-sought enemy they refused, excited by the prospect of glory: 'They held their position, unmoving, so those behind kept riding forward … they rode on in all their competitive pride, in no order, one in front of the other,

Edward III and his son Edward, the Prince of Wales. In Edward III the English armies of the period enjoyed the command of a young and vigorous king, a king who had honed his skills in difficult wars against the Scots in which he had learned important lessons in tactics, logistics and management. A much-vaunted figure both in England and abroad, Edward was often seen as a chivalric ideal, and though he gave the chroniclers of the time much to write about in that regard he was also an example of military competence. His blending of the period's very real sense of chivalry with a consciously professional approach to warfighting aptly balances some of the contradictions of the age. His son, first blooded at Crécy, would prove to be his father's match in both skill at war and the loyalty he could command from men both high-born and low. (© The British Library Board, Royal 20 D X f. 28)

until they saw the English arrayed in three well ordered battalions, waiting for them' (Bryant 2015: 180). The French army was hardly organized for battle, but the passion of the moment was forcing the matter, so while 'Philip lost his sang-froid, rapidly followed by his grip on events, Edward remained in control throughout' (Ayton 2005a: 106).

For the crossbowmen who were to lead the advance and provide cover for the succeeding waves of horsemen, the reality was more complex. Froissart observed that the Genoese 'would sooner have gone to the devil than fight at that moment, for they had just marched over eighteen miles [29km], in armour and carrying their crossbows' (Brereton 1978: 88). In addition, their headlong march meant that their pavises were buried deep in the baggage train, so they would have to advance across an open field, their eyes blinded by the lowering afternoon sun, shooting and reloading without any cover. The crossbowmen started out towards the English at 6pm; Froissart recounts how

The Genoese, having been marshalled
into proper order and made to advance, began to utter
loud whoops to frighten the English. The English waited in silence and did not stir. The Genoese hulloa'd a second time and advanced a little farther, but the English still made no move. Then they raised a third shout, very loud and clear, levelled their crossbows and began to shoot. (Brereton 1978: 88)

Geoffrey the Baker observed that

the trumpets blared, the drums and horns and clarions sounded, the French shouted at the English with the noise of thunder, and the French crossbow men started the battle. However none of their bolts reached the English but fell a long way short of them. Our archers were roused into action by the deafening shouts of the French crossbow men, and, piercing and killing the enemy with their arrows, they brought to an end the shower of bolts with a hailstorm of arrows. (Preest & Barber 2012: 73)

Jean le Bel agrees that battle was commenced by the advance of the crossbowmen towards the English line. His account (from the French

A pavise, made in Germany c.1385–87. Such large shields were common items of siege warfare and garrison defence throughout Europe, and had been for some considerable time. They also saw some use aboard ships (especially galleys), helping to deflect enemy archery aimed at the unprotected deck, and of course on the battlefield where they offered moveable cover for archers or crossbowmen. Owing to the exposed nature of a crossbowman during the reloading of his weapon, a pavisier (shield-bearer) would accompany him, setting the shield up to offer protection. A pavise could have iron points (as this one does) that were driven into the ground to help stabilize it, providing shelter for both pavisier and crossbowman. The disaster for the Genoese crossbowmen at Crécy seems to have been caused in large part because their pavises, piled up in the back of the baggage train, were unavailable to them, leaving them unprotected in their advance on the English line. (Metropolitan Museum of Art, www.metmuseum.org)

## Ottone Doria

Ottone Doria was born around 1300 into a well-established Genoese family with a reputation for the provision of warships and soldiers to the princes of the region. With a long history of piracy and mercenary service, Doria had supplied large numbers of ships, troops and crossbowmen to the French crown on a number of prior occasions. His success was mitigated somewhat by domestic issues when a new government arose in Genoa in 1340 that had little sympathy for Doria or his politics; leaving the city of his birth a year later for exile in France, he continued contracting men and ships from across Italy, albeit on a smaller scale as he was 'now little more than a recruiter of mercenaries' (Livingstone & Witzel 2005: 77). Towards the end of 1345, Philippe VI contracted Doria to raise 3,000 crossbowmen and a few ships (with his more successful Genoese countryman Carlo Grimaldi paid to raise an additional 7,000 crossbowmen), both forces to be available by April 1346. Contingents were sent to garrison towns like Calais and Harfleur, while the remainder were incorporated into the royal army's fateful attempt to catch Edward III. Ottone Doria was killed leading his crossbowmen at Crécy.

perspective) notes how the hasty and importunate beginning of the battle was ordered by

> the officers of the crossbowmen and the auxiliaries and Genoese [who] ordered their men to advance, and to go ahead of the lords' battalions initially and shoot at the English. They advanced so close that they were soon exchanging dense volleys, and it wasn't long before the Genoese and auxiliaries were thrown into disorder by the English archers and started to fly. (Bryant 2015: 180)

It seems likely that the 'auxiliaries', assuming they weren't the shieldless Genoese pavisiers, were also crossbowmen, possibly contracted troops, so the force that approached the English line could have been up to 5,000–6,000 strong, though lower figures are certainly possible (the chroniclers give numbers ranging from 2,000 up to over 6,000 for the Genoese alone, making almost no reference to the other crossbowmen who would certainly have been part of the royal army). The lack of their pavises, trapped in the baggage train, would certainly have counted against the Genoese, but the contention found in Jean de Venette's Chronicle and the *Grandes Chroniques de France* that a sudden burst of rain drenched their crossbows and slackened the strings seems rather fanciful; such strings were thick and well-waxed, and the Genoese (and one might presume the other crossbow contingents that may have accompanied them) were professionals who knew how to protect their expensive and well-maintained equipment. The reason why they broke was that they were advancing against an unintimidated, numerous and well-prepared enemy who could outrange and outshoot them. The disruptive effect of the arrowstorm, even up to 275m out from the English line, would have been considerable, and though the crossbowmen were well armoured their faces, arms and legs were mostly still vulnerable to wounds even at extreme range. The closer they came to the English the more powerful and accurate the enemy arrows would become, and with no real prospect of being able to shoot their way forward, retreat was the only sensible option.

Jean le Bel's description of the ensuing carnage is worth quoting at length because he heard about it directly from his patron, Sir John of Hainault,

## Sir John Chandos

Sir John Chandos was born around 1314 into an old Norman family in Derbyshire. Knighted by the king at the battle of La Capelle in 1339, Chandos was present at Sluys a year later, where the chronicler Henry Knighton credits him with successfully reconnoitring the French fleet at anchor, a characteristic ability also noted in Geoffrey the Baker's chronicle where Chandos' scouting ahead of the main army is mentioned several times. Such roles suggest his trustworthiness and martial proficiency, as well as keen intelligence and quick wits. By the time of the Crécy campaign Chandos enjoyed the full confidence of the king, being entrusted along with some fellow picked knights to guard the Prince of Wales during the battle. Certainly the place he occupied in the Prince of Wales's division gave Chandos plenty of opportunity to cover himself in glory and form a strong bond with the young prince; in subsequent campaigns Chandos played an important role, especially as a close adviser to the Prince of Wales during the Poitiers *chevauchée* ten years later. Eventually finding himself as seneschal of Poitou in 1369, Chandos was killed in a skirmish on a bridge over the River Vienne at Lussac, a death mourned by friends and foes alike.

who (with his retinue of 10–12 knights) was a key participant in the battle, and saw at first hand the disaster that befell the French. The advance of the Genoese and auxiliaries had failed, and they were falling back in disorder:

> But the great lords' battalions were so fired by their rivalry with one another that they didn't wait for each other but charged in a jumbled mass, with no order whatever, trapping the Genoese and auxiliaries between themselves and the English, so they couldn't flee but fell under the charging horses and were trampled by the seething horde behind – they were tumbling over each other like a vast litter of pigs. At the same time the English archers were loosing such awesome volleys that the horses were riddled by the dreadful barbed arrows; some refused to go on, others leapt wildly, some viciously lashed and kicked, others turned tail despite their masters' efforts, and others collapsed as the arrows struck, unable to endure. Then the English lords – who were dismounted – advanced and fell upon these men, as helpless as their horses. (Bryant 2015: 180)

The suggestion, prominent in Froissart, that the King of France (the Comte de Alençon in another version) demanded that the retreating Genoese be ridden down for their cowardice is possible, though it seems more likely that the terrible confusion of their retreat was caught in the impetuous charge of the first *bataille* who refused to wait any longer for their chance of glory.

The strength of a charge mostly lies in its discipline and cohesion, factors that were sacrificed from the very first. Nevertheless, the failure of the first cavalry assault did nothing to dissuade those who came in its wake. Charge after charge was launched, Geoffrey the Baker recording up to 15 separate attempts by the French cavalry (among three great assaults) to gain the top of the ridge and break through the young Prince of Wales's line. The chaos of the field could only increase with each subsequent attempt, with ever more horses killed or wounded, the bodies of the injured and the dead piling up in a suffocating press, and the remnants of retreating *batailles* disrupting the order of those who had just manoeuvred through the southern entrance to the valley and were trying to form up to launch their own assault. At no point was a change of tactics considered or employed, with rank after rank of horsemen

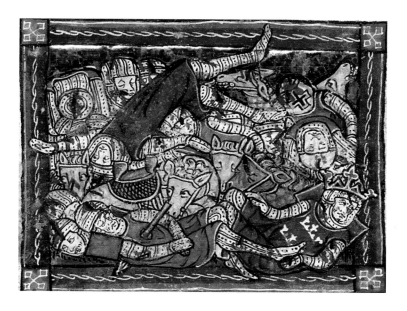

continuing to force their way through an increasingly awful mire of their brethren.

Even with the ready work of the archers it was developing into a lively evening for the Prince of Wales, locked as he was in the heart of the fight almost from its outset. Described by Geoffrey the Baker as a man of 'remarkable prowess', the young prince 'pierced horses and laid low their riders, shook helmets and broke off lances, and skilfully avoided blows aimed at himself … he gave an example to all his men of the right way to fight' (Preest & Barber 2012: 74). Some French attacks made it all the way up the ridge through the blizzard of arrows and threw themselves on the English men-at-arms. Geoffrey the Baker writes:

> At Crécy those few men drawn up against the enemy in the front line remained in place throughout the battle with the young prince, while the Frenchmen kept changing and waves of fresh, new soldiers kept coming against the English as they replaced the killed or the weary or the wounded who had withdrawn. Indeed their non-stop attacks kept the prince and his comrades so busy, that the prince was compelled to fight kneeling down against the masses of the enemy who poured around him. (Preest & Barber 2012: 74)

Geoffrey the Baker and Henry Knighton agree that over the course of the evening there were three great assaults: Knighton describes how the second major attack was led by 'two kings and a duke, namely the king of Bohemia, the king of Mallorca, and the duke of Lorraine, with many other noblemen' (Martin 1995: 63). Froissart takes up the tale of the blind Bohemian king:

> 'Sirs, ye are my men, my companions and friends in this enterprise; I require you bring me so forward that I may strike one stroke with my sword.' They said they would do his commandment; and to the intent that they should not lose him in the press, they tied all their reins of their bridles each to other, and set the king before to accomplish his desire; and so they went on their enemies … [the king] struck a stroke with his sword, yea and more than four, and fought valiantly. And so did his company, and they adventured themselves so forward that they were all slain, and the next day they were found in the place about the king, and all their horses tied each to other. (Ashley 1887: 103–04)

Such an ending, if true, would warm the cockles of any chivalrous heart, but apocryphal or not the King of Bohemia did fall that day, as did the

The chronicler Jean Froissart notes one of the more sanguinary characteristics of a medieval battlefield, occurring at Crécy as the battle was coming to its close: 'However, among the English there were pillagers and irregulars, Welsh and Cornishmen armed with long knives, who went out after the French (their own men-at-arms and archers making way for them) and, when they found any in difficulty, whether they were counts, barons, knights or squires, they killed them without mercy. Because of this, many were slaughtered that evening, regardless of their rank. It was a great misfortune and the king of England was afterwards very angry that none had been taken for ransom, for the number of dead lords was very great' (Brereton 1978: 93). (© The British Library Board, Additional 10294 f. 93)

An image of archers wearing various liveries, by James le Palmer from the *Omne Bonum*, c.1360–75. Throughout the period individuals as well as bodies of troops were beginning to use badges, signs and uniforms to distinguish themselves on battlefields where arms and armour were no great indicators of which side one was on. The most well-known examples among the English are the green-and-white livery of the archers of Cheshire and Flint for the Crécy campaign and the Prince of Wales's edict a decade later for his troops to wear a red cross on their clothing. In this image note the relatively advanced helmets and aventails worn by some of the bowmen. (© The British Library Board, Royal 6 E VI f. 183v)

King of Majorca, the Duke of Lorraine and scores of the most senior men in the Kingdom of France. The King of Bohemia's more pragmatic son Charles was also at the battle and was one of the few men of high rank to survive, mainly because he rode off the field when he saw how the fight was unfolding.

Knighton recounts that the third great attack was led by the King of France himself, in conjunction with Sir John of Hainault, where the French monarch 'was struck in the face by an arrow, and his charger was killed' (Martin 1995: 63). But it was all for nought. The best and strongest force of knights in Europe had ground themselves down to the bone in front of an implacable English army. Jean le Bel observed how

> The king was forced to leave, utterly distraught: against his wishes his men – including Sir John of Hainault, retained to preserve the king's life and honour – led him away; and they kept him riding through the night until they reached Labroye. There he stopped to rest, weighed down with grief, and rode next day to Amiens to wait for the rest of his army, or what was left of it. (Bryant 2015: 181)

Edward III, in his account of the battle given in his letter to Sir Thomas Lucy on 3 September, touches on the events of the day only in a circumspect manner, though he does make reference to 'a small area where the first onslaught occurred [and] more than 1500 knights and squires died, quite apart from those who died later elsewhere on the field' (quoted

For the French the defeat at Crécy caused them to re-evaluate the usefulness of their levies of rowdy, largely untrained militias: 'the common troops provided by the cities and towns, who had proved wholly ineffective on the battlefield, were no longer summoned in large numbers. In the following years, the king preferred to ask the towns to provide small contingents of well-equipped and well-trained sergeants and crossbowmen, rather than large numbers of infantry who were ill-disciplined and useless in a fight against professional soldiers' (Schnerb 2005: 271). (© The British Library Board, Royal 20 C VII f. 136)

in Barber 1986: 22). There is little doubt that the 'small area' was the ridge leading up to the Prince of Wales's position, where the crossbowmen failed and the French *batailles* came apart in confusion under storms of arrows.

The night passed quietly, with the following day given over to more fighting or sporadic mopping-up (depending on which chronicler one chooses to believe), followed by a reckoning of the dead. The battle proved to be a bloody ruin for the French aristocracy, in part because there was little quarter given on either side, with no prisoners of note being taken. It is as difficult to find reliable figures for the number of casualties as it is participants in a medieval battle, and Crécy is no exception. Lord Northburgh put the noble French dead at a realistic 1,542 (with no mention of men-at-arms or the rest); the *Lanercost Chronicle* assumes a much more sanguinary 20,000 dead; Jean le Bel thought the knightly casualties numbered 1,200 knights, with 15,000–16,000 others on top of that; Henry Knighton estimated 2,000 men-at-arms and 32,000 others perished; while Geoffrey the Baker states that 'The total of knights and men of higher ranks killed in that battle was more than four thousand. As for the men of other ranks killed there, no one took the trouble to count them' (Preest & Barber 2012: 75).

# Poitiers

## 19 September 1356

## BACKGROUND TO BATTLE

The years following the Crécy campaign were peppered with raids and engagements of varying consequence, none of which altered the basic tenor of an English ascendancy over a weakened France. As the historian Bertrand Schnerb observes:

> The battle of Crécy brought with it the destruction of the French army and a political crisis that prevented an effective military retaliation, with the result that the English were able to establish a lasting presence in Calais ... The defeat at Crécy would not have been the 'hard blow' that it was for the monarchy were it not for the fact that it served to reveal a profound political malaise. (Schnerb 2005: 285–86)

Despite the internal strife that surrounded his throne, Jean II (who had succeeded his unhappy father in 1350) had not buckled to Edward III's demand for lands and the settlement of his rights in Aquitaine in the abortive Treaty of Guînes (1354). The French refusal to come to heel guaranteed that the English king would press his claim once again at the point of a sword.

Two *chevauchées* were launched in 1355, a frustratingly inconclusive outing from Calais by King Edward himself (before yet more problems caused by the ever-troublesome Scots drew him back to England) and a far more destructive affair by his warlike son in the Languedoc, the first independent command for the young prince. The Prince of Wales was 'generous, proud, forceful and fierce, characteristics well-suited to the leader of an Anglo-Gascon *chevauchée*' (Rogers 2000: 294); but despite his willingness to fight, he had failed to draw the French into battle, with Jean le Bel observing in despair how the

A scene from the *Chroniques de France ou de St Denis* showing a battle on a bridge over the Seine. Composed sometime after 1380, the illustration shows some of the fashionable changes in arms and armour (such as jupons and bascinets with 'hounskull'-style visors), but also an archer and crossbowman who, in a fit of artistic even-handedness, appear to have shot one another. Both are notable for the padded gambesons they wear, as well as the crossbowman's bascinet and aventail, the archer's kettle-style hat and the archer's sword – examples of the fact that light foot troops became increasingly well-armed and armoured as the war progressed. (© The British Library Board, Royal 20 C VII f. 137v)

French army did nothing but dog the Black Prince's footsteps: 'still the French lords followed them but made no attack despite having an army three times as strong, for which they were sorely reproached. I don't know what stopped them attacking the rearguard at the very least, unless they were enchanted or bewitched' (Bryant 2015: 223). The Black Prince did not rest on his hard-won laurels, launching a series of raids in the succeeding months, bringing even more of Gascony to heel in the teeth of the local French lords. As the summer of 1356 approached, King Edward was to return to Calais and Henry of Lancaster to Brittany, re-igniting the war in the north, while the Black Prince was to ride north from Bergerac towards the Loire where 'the wealthy cities of Limoges, Bourges, Tours, and Poitiers all lay within reach' (Rogers 2000: 351), razing all in his path as he searched for a French army to fight.

Things went well. No French force of any significance dared come close to the prince's army, leaving it free to rampage about the countryside far and wide for weeks according to the *Anonimalle Chronicle*, 'burning and devastating the counties of Périgord and Limousin and all the country of French Gascony; the county of la Marche, the city of Issoudun belonging to the king of France; and all the land of the Duchy of Berry … burning and destroying up to the town of Romorantin' (Rogers 1999: 164). Hearing of the Black Prince's depredations, Jean II had begun marshalling his army at Chartres and Orléans, arriving at the former on 28 August with the intention of marching towards Tours and catching the Anglo-Gascons in a battle, a piece of information that soon reached Prince Edward's ears: '"at this," the *Eulogium Historiarum* tells us, "he rejoiced greatly"' (quoted in Rogers 2000: 357) and made for Tours as well.

Arriving at Romorantin on 30 August, the Prince of Wales tarried for several days awaiting the arrival of King Edward with a relieving force which never came; soon enough news came that the King of France was on the move once more, Geoffrey the Baker noting how 'the prince, who was eager for war because of the peace which always follows war, moved camp towards the crowned one [Jean II]' (Preest & Barber 2012: 121). The two sides shadowed each other on either side of the Loire towards Tours, the Anglo-Gascons trying to provoke a French response, and the French in turn trying to find a way either to trap the Anglo-Gascons or to cut off their line of retreat. It was for this reason that Jean II finally crossed the Loire at Blois, forcing Prince Edward to fall back south to ensure that the Valois king didn't outmanoeuvre him. Unable to outpace the French, Prince Edward knew he could not guarantee a line of retreat to Bordeaux, meaning that 'the Valois would

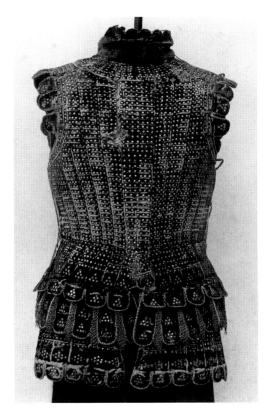

An Italian-made brigandine from around the middle of the 15th century. Armour such as this (if of a rather less elaborate manufacture) and the jack-of-plates became much more common as the 14th century progressed, with the jack-of-plates becoming popular among all classes of soldiery. Brigandines and jacks-of-plate were designed on the same principle – the fitting of serried ranks of small plates of armour within a jerkin or doublet, though with a brigandine such plates were riveted rather sewn into the fabric. Both brigandines and jacks-of-plate would be worn over a mail shirt and gambeson, affording the wearer considerable protection. (Metropolitan Museum of Art, www.metmuseum.org)

have the opportunity to try and hold him in place until he starved or was forced to take the tactical initiative, which considering the disparity in force between the two sides would doubtless have been disastrous' (Rogers 2000: 366). Offering battle in such a situation was a gamble; fortunately for Edward, Jean II was minded to fight, Jean le Bel observing that 'When he knew for certain that he was so close to the English, he felt sure they would wait to face him' (Bryant 2015: 226).

One day after a hard skirmish on Saturday 17 September, the Prince of Wales advanced on King Jean II le Bon's position near Poitiers, arrayed for battle. The Cardinal of Périgord shuttled between the two armies for most of Sunday and early Monday in a fruitless attempt to broker a truce that might appeal to the Prince of Wales in part because of the perceived weakness of the Anglo-Gascon army 'as they were few in number, away from home in a strange land and pitifully worn out with the toil of their marches. Also they would be fighting against large numbers of French citizens, defending their own soil, and refreshed by receiving from their thoughtful leader all necessary provisions and a long period of rest' (Preest & Barber 2012: 124). For the Black Prince, who had been actively seeking battle, a truce on any but the most favourable terms was pointless, however. For the French a truce would at best postpone their problems, whereas a victory – not unlikely considering the balance of forces – could reap them significant rewards. Finally Jean II was persuaded, saying 'We do not wish for [Prince Edward] to depart without a battle. Now we shall see if he can stand against us in our own land and resist our power' (quoted in Rogers 2000: 371).

**MAP KEY**

**1** The French and Anglo-Gascon armies sit opposite one another for some time, neither one wishing to lose the advantage by being the first to make a move. Finally, movement in the Anglo-Gascon force suggesting that the Prince of Wales is attempting to retreat from the field provokes the French into an assault. Marshal Arnoul d'Audrehem's cavalry attack the Earl of Warwick's position while Marshal Clermont's cavalry attack the Earl of Salisbury's position. Both act in support of the first *bataille* led by the Constable of France; like the rest of the French host – with the exception of Clermont and d'Audrehem's cavalry detachments – the Constable's *bataille* has abandoned its horses and advances on foot. Both cavalry elements as well as the first *bataille* are thrown back, with d'Audrehem taken prisoner and both Clermont and the Constable of France killed.

**2** The second *bataille* under the Dauphin attacks the Anglo-Gascon positions, engaging in heavy fighting for up to two hours, but fails to breach the line. After suffering heavy casualties the Dauphin's *bataille* makes an orderly retreat.

**3** In a much-debated scandalous act, the *bataille* of the duc d'Orléans abandons the field without engaging the Anglo-Gascons at all. Its flight provokes some of the Black Prince's troops (especially from the Earl of Warwick's division) to launch a pursuit.

**4** King Jean II le Bon appears on the field with his *bataille*, moving to attack. Despite being disheartened by the unexpected arrival and size of the French host, the tired Anglo-Gascon force led by the Prince of Wales advances to meet the threat, sending a 160-strong force of mounted archers and men-at-arms led by the Captal de Buch on a wide flanking attack.

**5** The French seem to be gaining the upper hand over the exhausted Anglo-Gascons until the Earl of Warwick's returning troops take the King of France's *bataille* in the flank, soon followed by the Captal de Buch's mixed cavalry force which attacks in the rear, causing a general French collapse. King Jean II le Bon and his youngest son Philippe are taken prisoner.

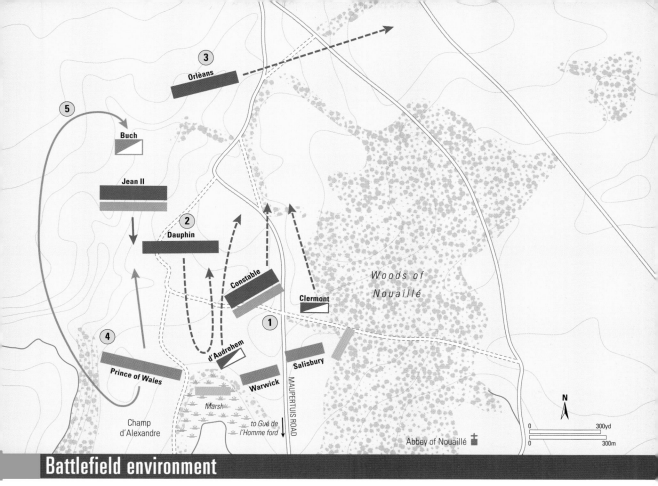

Orléans
3

5

Buch

Jean II

2
Dauphin

Constable

Clermont

Woods of
Nouaillé

1

4

d'Audrehem

Salisbury

Prince of Wales

Warwick

MAUPERTUIS ROAD

Champ
d'Alexandre

Marsh

to Gué de
l'Homme ford

N

Abbey of Nouaillé

0        300yd
0        300m

## Battlefield environment

There is much disagreement as to the exact location of the fighting on the Poitiers battlefield, though it is certain that it took place in the immediate vicinity of the Nouaillé wood. Robert Hardy follows the approach of the historian Clifford Rogers, whose interpretations in turn follow those 'suggested by [J.M.] Tourneur-Aumont [in his 1940 book *La Bataille de Poitiers 1356*], who positions the main fight rather to the south and west of the usually accepted site' (Strickland & Hardy 2005: 299). The terrain was well chosen for a defensive battle, being in many places marshy, rough and broken, forcing the French horse and foot to attack through ground that was narrow and unfavourable. The

Nouaillé wood formed the eastern border of the battlefield; running parallel to the wood was the Maupertuis road, along which ran dense hedgerows, following the road as it descended south into the marshes, and it was along this line that the divisions of the Earl of Salisbury and the Earl of Warwick would do much of their fighting; the southern edge of the field was defined by the twists of the River Miosson and the swathes of marshy ground that could be found along its banks; a small hill which stood to the south and west of the woods, its flanks and rear protected by the Miosson, would serve as the position of Prince Edward's division for most of the battle.

**OPPOSITE** A photograph of the northern part of the field of Poitiers, sometimes referred to as the field of Nouaillé-Maupertuis in French sources, looking towards the woods of Nouaillé which formed a border along the eastern extent of the battlefield. Though there have undoubtedly been changes to the landscape in the intervening centuries, the undulating nature of the ground with its rough and broken patches is consistent with the contemporary descriptions of the scene. The original hawthorn hedgerows, such a feature of the battle, have mostly disappeared, though Robert Hardy in his many walks of the site states that there are still some ancient and thorny remnants to be found. (Ludovic Bonneaud)

# INTO COMBAT

Jean le Bel noted how the Anglo-Gascons resolved to fight and 'would all risk a good death by selling their lives dearly if that was Our Lord's will. So they drew up their battalions in fine and shrewdly marshalled order' (Bryant 2015: 227). The Black Prince's army comprised 2,000 archers, 3,000 men-at-arms and around 1,000 other foot troops (some of whom were likely Gascon crossbowmen) according to Sir Bartholomew Burghersh, a Knight of the Garter who had fought with his prince at Crécy and would so again at Poitiers (Strickland & Hardy 2005: 299–300). The first division was under Thomas Beauchamp, Earl of Warwick, and John de Vere, Earl of Oxford; the second division was under the Prince of Wales; the third division was under William Montague, Earl of Salisbury, and Robert Ufford, Earl of Suffolk. Other men of note present at the battle were Jean III de Grailly, the Captal de Buch, who was a Gascon and a loyal lieutenant of Edward's in Aquitaine, and Sir John Chandos, a close associate of the Black Prince's who had fought by his side at Crécy.

The possible numbers for the French army vary more widely, but on balance it most likely consisted of 10,000–12,000 men-at-arms, 2,000 crossbowmen and 2,000 more foot troops, organized into a covering vanguard and four *batailles*. The vanguard consisted of a mixed force of men-at-arms, crossbowmen and foot troops as well as two cavalry elements (made up from the 300–500 best and most heavily armoured horsemen in the army) led by Marshal Arnoul d'Audrehem and Marshal Jean de Clermont. The first *bataille* was led by Gautier VI de Brienne, duc d'Athènes and Constable of France; the second was led by the king's eldest son the Dauphin, Charles, duc de Normandie; the third by the king's brother Philippe de Valois, duc d'Orléans; and the fourth by the king himself, with the famed knight Geoffrey de Charny bearing his banner (Rogers 2000: 376–77).

The advice given to the King of France as recorded by Froissart was to advance 'with everyone on foot, except for three hundred of the most vigorous and experienced knights in your army, mounted on first rate horses, to break through those archers and scatter them. And then your formations of men-at-arms would follow quickly on foot and engage their men at arms hand-to-hand' (Brereton 1978: 128). Jean le Bel records the French decision 'that they should all fight on foot, for fear of the archers who always killed their horses, as at the battle of Crécy' (Bryant 2015: 226), though Geoffrey the Baker thought such 'shocking madness' was the result of the king giving too much weight to the advice of Scottish knight Lord William Douglas, who was in attendance with 200 of his countrymen.

The two armies faced one another, neither willing to make the first move and thus lose the tactical advantage. Finally, either as a feint to draw in the French or perhaps from a genuine desire to leave the field, the Anglo-Gascon force began to move. The Black Prince wrote that 'Because we were short of supplies and for other reasons, it was agreed that we should retreat in a flanking movement, so that if they wanted to attack or to approach us in a position which was not in any way greatly to our disadvantage we would give battle' (quoted in Barber 1986: 58). Whatever the truth of the matter it provoked the French into action, for once they lost sight of Prince Edward's banner Geoffrey the Baker noted how 'they concluded that the prince was

fleeing from the scene' (Preest & Barber 2012: 126) and the vanguard, driven by Marshal d'Audrehem's desire to exploit what he thought was a retreat, moved to attack.

The Black Prince had moved his division onto a hill by the French right where, as Geoffrey the Baker recounts, 'In the protection given by this place they easily concealed themselves among the bushes, looking down on the enemy from above'; the commands of Warwick and Salisbury were to Prince Edward's right

> by a long hedge and ditch, with one of its ends running down into the marsh. The earl of Warwick, the leader and commander of the first division, held the slope where it ran down into the marsh. In the higher section of the hedge, some distance away from where it ran down into the marsh, there was an open cutting or gap which carters made in the autumn, and the third division under the earl of Salisbury was stationed a stone's throw from this gap. (Preest & Barber 2012: 126)

By moving to the hill the Black Prince could give cover to his remaining divisions if they were to move south off the field along the Maupertuis road, as the Earl of Warwick's division had in fact started to do, crossing the Miosson at the Gué de l'Homme ford. It seems likely it was the movement of the Black Prince's banner as he repositioned his force on the hill that sparked the French assault.

Marshal d'Audrehem's cavalry struck towards the Earl of Warwick's position, while Marshal Clermont, far from convinced of the wisdom of such a hasty French move but stung into action by the mockery of d'Audrehem and others, took his horsemen towards gaps in the hedgerows by the Earl of Salisbury's position at the other end of the Anglo-Gascon line in an outflanking manoeuvre. Geoffrey the Baker reports how the Earl of Salisbury 'cleverly guessed his purpose, and so it was that the commander of our rearguard who sustained the first shock of battle, as he sought speedily to close the gap in the hedge and so prevent the enemy from crossing through it' (Preest & Barber 2012: 127). It seems that the rest of the first *bataille*, led by the Constable of France, marched in support of the two marshals against the whole of the Anglo-Gascon line, with ranks of crossbowmen to the fore providing some cover for the main force of dismounted men-at-arms.

The Earl of Salisbury met Clermont's attack, forcing it back on its heels with the help of his well-sited archers whom Geoffrey the Baker notes were 'positioned behind a safe rampart above the ditch and beyond the hedge, [where] they made arrows prevail over soldiers in armour, as the bolts from the crossbow men flew ever more thickly and frequently' (Preest & Barber 2012: 127). Marshal Clermont was among the fallen. Meanwhile to the south, the Earl of Warwick had seen d'Audrehem's advance and re-crossed the Miosson at the Gué de l'Homme ford to meet the attack. Initially the archers, positioned as they were along the marshy banks of the Miosson, proved of little use against the heavily armoured French men-at-arms or their barded horses who were screening the Constable's *bataille*, as Geoffrey the Baker recounts:

> The French cavalry, who were ordered to ride down our archers and so protect their own side from arrows, remained stationary next to their own men, and offered to our archers breasts so strongly protected by steel plates and stout shields that the arrows shot were either broken into pieces by those hard objects or deflected up to the heavens. (Preest & Barber 2012: 127)

The Earl of Oxford, seeing the problem, left his position and led the archers to the flank of the French cavalry, where their shafts could find softer targets. Geoffrey the Baker again:

> He ordered them to shoot their arrows from here into the hind-quarters of the horses. A soon as this was done, the wounded warhorses kicked and trampled on their riders, and then, turning back against their own men, caused great havoc among the French lords, who had quite a different end in mind. Then, once the archers had driven back the warhorses, they returned to their original position and shot their arrows straight ahead into the fighting flanks of the French. (Preest & Barber 2012: 127)

Both cavalry attacks were repulsed, Froissart observing how 'The battalion of the Marshals was soon after put to the rout by the arrows of the archers, and the assistance of the men-at-arms, who rushed amongst them as they were struck down, and seized and slew them at their pleasure' (quoted in Nicolle 2004: 61). With his cavalry broken Marshal d'Audrehem, already wounded, was taken prisoner while Lord Douglas, who had ridden into battle alongside him, was also grievously injured and had to be dragged from the field by his few remaining countrymen, the remainder of his Scottish contingent having been cut to pieces.

Geoffrey the Baker told of how 'There was no break now in war's grim madness. Those lions, the earls of Warwick and Salisbury, competed to see which of them could flood the soil of Poitou with more draughts of French blood, and which of them could boast that his weapons were more deeply stained with the warm blood of Frenchmen' (Preest & Barber 2012: 127). With the failure of the cavalry the archers were free to play havoc among the Constable's men who were heavily engaged with Warwick's and Salisbury's divisions. The fierceness of the fighting cost the French dearly and with the death of the Constable at the heart of the maelstrom the first *bataille* lost the will to carry on, Geoffrey the Baker observing that 'war's fierce fury ... had compelled all the others of that French first array to go down the road of an honourable death or a compulsory flight' (Preest & Barber 2012: 128).

An illustration showing the death of Gautier VI de Brienne, duc d'Athènes and Constable of France. An interesting and cosmopolitan man, Gautier was a descendant of the famous John of Brienne, king of Jerusalem at the height of the Crusades. His fame was well-rewarded with the position of Constable, the most senior soldier in the army short of the king himself, but his actions at Poitiers, following on the heels of the advance guard led by Clermont and d'Audrehem, were inauspicious. (© The British Library Board, Royal 14 E V f. 499v)

The second *bataille*, approximately 4,000 men strong and led by the King of France's eldest son, the Dauphin, Charles, duc de Normandie, advanced through the confused and retreating ranks of the now shattered first line. They were unsupported by cavalry and presumably had few crossbowmen to counter the threat of the English archers, the majority having been a part of the now collapsed first *bataille*. The Anglo-Gascon line they were approaching had been reinforced by the Prince of Wales's division, which had moved from its position on the hill down to the hedge line in direct support of the Earl of Warwick's men. Though Geoffrey the Baker notes that 'the appearance of this array was more terrible and more frightening than the face of the first array' (Preest & Barber 2012: 128), the reality was that the Anglo-Gascons were still in a strongly defensible position with mostly fresh troops that were flushed from their recent victory over the vanguard. The advancing ranks of close-packed French men-at-arms soaked up showers of English arrows, Froissart observing that 'If the truth must be told, the English archers were a huge asset to their side and a terror to the French; their shooting was so heavy and accurate that the French did not know where to turn to avoid their arrows' (Brereton 1978: 135).

The clash was more intense and long-lasting than the one which had preceded it, perhaps lasting up to two hours as the Dauphin's men battled to try to force their way through the gaps in the thick hawthorn hedgerows. Knighton's account gives the image of an intense and wearing fight:

> The second line of the French came and engaged the prince of Wales, and they fought bitterly under cover of a hedgerow, and the English were exhausted by the intensity of the battle, and their weapons much worn. And so strong and hard was the fight that the archers ran out of arrows, and picked up stones, and fought

with swords and lances, and anything that they could find, and they defended themselves with marvellous courage, and at last as God willed it the French took flight. (Martin 1995: 145)

The Dauphin's *bataille*, harried and weakened by the English archers and unable to pierce the Anglo-Gascon hedge line, suffered greatly, with the duc de Bourbon, the King of France's brother, killed and the Dauphin's standard-bearer seized in the close-pressed fray.

Geoffrey the Baker recounted, somewhat smugly, how the Dauphin's *bataille* gave up the fight: 'Although this second French array resisted our men for longer than the first array, yet, after a great number of them had been killed, they wisely took that cautious step which the French, invincible in argument, are accustomed to call not a flight but a retreat to a fair position' (Preest & Barber 2012: 128). In fairness to the Dauphin it seems his *bataille* did consciously disengage from the fight and make an orderly retreat rather than break and run away; the same could not be said for his uncle Philippe de Valois, duc d'Orléans, commander of the third *bataille*.

The chronicles are confused as to why what followed happened, whether by the King of France's order, a misunderstanding, or worse. Whatever the reason, as the Dauphin's *bataille* retreated from the field that of the duc d'Orléans joined him, quitting the battle without ever having engaged the enemy. Despite the fact that some among Orléans' command (including the French king's youngest son) did come back and rejoin their monarch, the majority did not, depriving the French of a vital body of fresh troops at a point in the battle when their contribution could have been most telling. Jonathan Sumption notes that 'After the battle, when reputations were at stake, it was put about that this too had happened by John II's order. But no one believed it. "Wretches and cowards" [the Italian chronicler Matteo] Villani called them, echoing the outrage of most Frenchmen' (Sumption 1999: 242).

Geoffrey the Baker noted the toll that the hours of fighting had taken on the weary Anglo-Gascon force:

Meanwhile our men placed their wounded under bushes and hedges. Others snatched from the conquered enemy spears and swords which were more in one piece than their own broken weapons, and archers hurried to pull out arrows from half-alive wretches. There was no one who was not wounded or exhausted from the extreme effort of the day, apart only from the four hundred men serving under the prince's banner, who were being kept in reserve to meet the crowned one [Jean II] and his division. (Preest & Barber 2012: 129)

The discipline that had kept the Anglo-Gascon troops in their positions was weakening, with the flight of the third *bataille* giving many the sense that the day was won; thus 'large numbers of troops (particularly from Warwick's division) had broken their formations to pursue the remnants of Orléans' force and take prisoners' (Rogers 2000: 381). It was at this point, Knighton recounts, that 'as the English stood refreshing themselves … there came King Jean of France with a huge force, directing his attack towards the prince, who had few men with him at that moment, because the rest were pursuing the defeated enemy' (Martin 1995: 145).

The appearance of the King of France's *bataille*, 'broad and very deep' (Bryant 2015: 227) according to Jean le Bel, sent a shockwave through the Anglo-Gascons. Geoffrey the Baker noted that 'It was not only the numbers of the enemy which terrified our men, but also the thought that our power had been considerably reduced. For besides the fact that the many wounded on our side were necessarily now out of the conflict, almost all the rest were very tired indeed, and the archers had used up their arrows' (Preest & Barber 2012: 129). The Captal de Buch, seeing the King of France's host, rode away with 60 men-at-arms and 100 mounted archers, further dismaying those who were left to face the approaching French. Sir John Chandos turned to the Prince, saying 'Ride forward, sir, the day is yours. God will be with you today. Let us make straight for your adversary the King of France, for it is there that the battle will be decided. I am certain that his valour will not allow him to flee' (Nicolle 2004: 69).

The Anglo-Gascon force marched out to meet Jean II, both sides letting loose their archers and crossbowmen as the forces approached one another, so that 'the threatening mass of French crossbowmen brought back grim night to the battlefield with the thick darkness of their bolts, but the darkness was repelled by the deadly shower of arrows shot by the young English archers, driven by desperation to frenzied resistance' (Preest & Barber 2012: 130). Soon enough the English archers had shot their last arrows and took their

# The attack of the Captal de Buch

The scene shows the moment when the small flanking force led by Jean III de Grailly, Captal de Buch, launches its attack. Followed by 60 men-at-arms and 100 mounted archers, de Grailly rode through dead ground around the right flank of the King of France's *bataille*, Geoffrey the Baker observing that he 'went round the battlefield without being seen and came to the low-lying place of the first station of the crowned one [Jean II]. Then he climbed to higher parts of the field along a path last trodden by the French, so that, suddenly breaking forth from his concealment, he showed us by the holy ensigns of St George that a friend was there' (Preest & Barber 2012: 130). Already heavily engaged with the Prince of Wales's division to the front, Jean II's men had just suffered a flank attack by the Earl of Warwick's men, newly returned to the field after their pursuit of the retreating Dauphin and the duc d'Orléans;

they were completely unaware of – and unprepared for – the new threat posed by the Captal de Buch. Jean III de Grailly's standard-bearer Elijah de Pommiers has raised the banner of St George; the archers, having quickly dismounted, are forming a line and are already starting to loose volleys of arrows into the backs of the Frenchmen who are perhaps less than 100m away; the Captal de Buch, raising his sword in the air, calls for his mounted men-at-arms to charge. Though his numbers are small the Captal de Buch was attacking the weakest point of the French formation, probably made up of 'men who had already been defeated under the constable, the dauphin, or as part of Orléans' force' (Rogers 2000: 383). The shock of mounted men-at-arms crashing into their backs to the accompaniment of showers of arrows was more than such men could take. Jean II's force began to break apart.

An image of some potentially valuable English prisoners from the *Chroniques de France ou de St Denis*. Jean II proved to be a handsome prize for the English, bringing in a £500,000 ransom (two decades' worth of revenue), and though he was the most valuable prize on offer, fortunes could still be made from the capture of lesser mortals: 'the Duke of Alençon brought £26,666; and Bertrand du Guesclin, the low-born soldier who became Constable of France, brought 100,000 francs (about £11,000). Lesser knights brought lesser sums, but still enough to make capturing them far preferable to killing them' (Rogers 1993: 256). (© The British Library Board, Royal 20 C VII f. 138v)

place beside the men-at-arms, carrying swords and leather shields and joining in the fray which quickly proved to be a violent and close-cut struggle. The Anglo-Gascon line was pushed back by the weight of the French men-at-arms, according to Knighton: 'But just as the French line bore down, the earl of Warwick returned from the chase with his whole force, and took the French army in the flank and fought them fiercely' (Martin 1995: 145). At about this time the Captal de Buch, riding with his small force through dead ground on a wide outflanking manoeuvre, fell on the rear lines of the King of France's *bataille*, Geoffrey the Baker recounting their devastating effect: 'The unhappy French were now attacked on both sides, for in their rear they were being cut down by the Captal de Buch's armed knights and pierced by the dread hail of the archers assigned to him. So then the whole formation of the French was cut to pieces' (Preest & Barber 2012: 131).

The rear ranks of the King of France's *bataille*, probably manned by those who had already been through the mill as part of the Constable's and Dauphin's forces, broke under this fresh assault (Rogers 2000: 383). Panic spread as the French force started to splinter, leading to ever-more ferocious attacks

A highly romanticized 19th-century imagining of Jean II's youngest son, Philippe de France, defending his besieged father at Poitiers moments before they are both captured. All four of the King's sons had been at the battle; Jean II's eldest son, the 18-year-old Dauphin, Charles, duc de Normandie, had led the second *bataille*, while Louis, duc d'Anjou, Jean, duc de Berry, and Philippe were either with the king or his brother, the soon-to-be disgraced duc d'Orléans. After the repulse of the Dauphin's attack it seems that the king ordered his younger sons to safety (a sensible enough precaution in dynastic times), and some interpret confusion over this order to be the reason for the duc d'Orléans' withdrawal from the field, 'escorting' the princes of the realm out of reach of the Anglo-Gascons. Despite this manoeuvre some of the duc d'Orléans' men, including the 14-year-old Philippe, broke away from his fast-retreating force to rejoin the king for the decisive stage of the battle. (Internet Archive)

by the Anglo-Gascon men-at-arms. Soon enough Jean II's standard-bearer Sir Geoffrey de Charny was surrounded and killed, and the French king himself seized as a prisoner along with his son; his army fell apart and was routed from the field 'pursued now by the Plantagenets, all the way to the gates of Poitiers' (Rogers 2000: 383). The Prince of Wales's victory, far from a foregone conclusion, was complete and emphatic. It would have a seismic impact on the French state, and though it would eventually give the English most of what they desired in the Treaty of Brétigny (1360), it would not be the end of their wars in France. Jean le Bel, considering the enormity of the Black Prince's triumph over the King of France and his nobles, acknowledged the scale of what had happened, observing that 'in all the history of Christendom no adventure so great ever befell so few' (Bryant 2015: 228).

# Analysis

## SLUYS

The merits of the initial French position taken by the French admirals Quiéret and Béhuchet, their fleet lying chained close to shore and awaiting attack, are arguable, but their over-hasty reaction to the English feint (a sign of their inexperience in such commands) destroyed the mutually supportive cohesion that their ships enjoyed, allowing the English to make the most of their more manoeuvrable vessels that also had the advantage of the wind. Edward III's innovative use of men-at-arms closely supported by massed archers was translated from land warfare to the sea with great effect; the sheer volume of arrows that ships full of bowmen could lay down on a target vessel made it very difficult for the French to keep the other ships bristling with Edward's men-at-arms at a safe distance. Another consideration pointed out by Rogers was that 'in a naval battle, unlike a land one, Edward could take the tactical offensive without disadvantage' (Rogers 2000: 191).

A significant factor in the English victory must be the relative paucity of well-trained troops on the French ships; if, as the *Grandes Chroniques de France* suggests, the vast majority were sailors rather than dedicated men-at-arms (or professional crossbowmen, the value of whom in such a battle was obvious), they would likely be less heavily armed and armoured, not to mention less experienced than the men who boarded their ships.

Jean le Bel's observation that 'The King of France has never again had such domination of the sea; the noble King Edward has ever since been its sovereign prince' (Bryant 2015: 86) was not really true even in the short term, but the damage done to French maritime capabilities was undeniable, and it certainly helped Edward in his prosecution of cross-Channel campaigns in the years to come. Despite such advantages the enormity of such a victory at sea didn't translate to Edward's campaigns on the land, and it was on land alone that he would need to bring his enemy to heel.

# CRÉCY

The English objective of the campaign was to 'undermine the political support of the Valois monarchy by showing its military weakness … to destroy the resources with which the Valois fought the war' (Rogers 1999: 266), and to draw the King of France into battle. The mixture of large bodies of archers with resolute men-at-arms, all dismounted in support of one another and on well-chosen ground, provided an iron-hard rock against which the French threw themselves repeatedly. That the English tactics worked as well as they did does owe something to the insistence of the French to play their part in Edward's battle plan.

Schnerb's contention that for the French army 'In this defeat, the tactical circumstances were more important than any weaknesses in military organisation' (Schnerb 2005: 271) has some validity; though the general quality of their foot soldiers was poor, there were enough mercenary and contract troops – and certainly more than enough mounted knights and men-at-arms – to cause such a relatively small English force considerable trouble. This is not to say that the French were thus incompetent or hidebound; the use of the Genoese crossbowmen as the vanguard at Crécy was meant to suppress the English archers and soften up the foot troops while the ranks of French knights organized themselves for the main assault, a sensible but rushed and ill-executed plan. The difficulty of command, shown by the French king's inability to control when to join battle, may well have been exacerbated by the awkward approach the French had to make to achieve the field, and the fact that they were transitioning from a long march straight into a deployment. It seems that after the initial confusion of whether to fight or not, the disastrous march of the crossbowmen compounded by the riotous mess the French men-at-arms made of their first charge, the course of the battle was set.

As might be expected after such a defeat there was some evolution in French tactics, with the habit of men-at-arms fighting on foot taking a firm hold, the mounted troops taking a more circumspect approach to their role on the battlefield by attacking the flanks and rear of enemy forces only when fortuitous openings presented themselves, and an increase in their numbers of crossbowmen and archers (Schnerb 2005: 271–72). The attempt to balance out the potency of the longbowmen was never fully realized, perhaps in part because there was no commensurate tactical evolution alongside the increase in numbers that would mitigate the greater range and stopping power enjoyed by the English archers. That a more wholesale evolution of French arms did not occur is understandable in as much as the defeat at Crécy, though shattering in scale, was not seen as part of a growing pattern of tactical change but rather as an isolated event, one that shamed France rather than educated it.

An illustration of a siege from the *Chroniques de France ou de St Denis*. The 'Edwardian' phase of the Hundred Years' War was unusual to the degree in which it was a mobile conflict; sieges, such as the one undertaken at Calais in the wake of Crécy in 1346–47, were uncharacteristic, though they would be a much more significant part of the subsequent phase of the war during 1369–89. The image has a good representation of crossbowmen, who arguably played a more important role in both sides of siege warfare than archers did, loading and shooting from behind a pavise. (© The British Library Board, Royal 20 C VII f. 24v)

A representation of King Jean II arrayed for war on a gold franc, minted sometime between 1350 and 1364. Though hardly a supporter of the French monarch (whom he insisted on calling 'the crowned one' due to his 'illegitimate' claim on King Edward III's French throne), Geoffrey the Baker does allow Jean II a moment of knightly grace in his conversation at supper with Prince Edward in the aftermath of his capture: 'although we are the prisoner of our noble cousin by the rights of war, yet we were not taken lurking in a corner like criminals or fainthearted fugitives, but, like noble knights ready to live or die for justice's sake, we were taken from our field of battle by the arbitrament of war. The rich were taken prisoner and kept for ransom, the despicable cowards ran away, and the bravest gave up their lives magnificently' (Preest & Barber 2012: 133). (Metropolitan Museum of Art, www.metmuseum.org)

# POITIERS

Strategically, the English and Anglo-Gascon *chevauchées* (King Edward's from Calais, Lancaster's from Brittany and the Black Prince's from Bordeaux) could cause immense damage individually or, by combining somewhere around the Loire, present the King of France with an enemy force of a potency not seen since Crécy. Such a meeting between English armies, however desirable, was unlikely due to the poor communications and logistics of the age. Nevertheless, the threat it presented to the French king could not be shrugged off. Jean II's engagement with the Black Prince's *chevauchée*, dogging his trail and trying to trap his army, forcing it to starve or fight on unfavourable terms, was sensible and certainly came close to working. The willingness of the Black Prince to entertain the entreaties of the Cardinal of Périgord on the eve of battle suggests that he knew that, although he had sought out a battle with the King of France, to fight in such a circumstance, with his line of retreat vulnerable to the slightest French manoeuvre, was a great risk. For Jean II in the end the urge to bring his enemy low before he could slip away outweighed any more circumspect strategy.

The French decision to attack mostly on foot made sense based on their previous experience at the hands of the English, but such formations need protection by cavalry (the dearth of any mounted protection was particularly disastrous for the King of France's *bataille*) and the support of large numbers of archers or crossbowmen if they are to hold their own against a competent foe. The use of crossbowmen in the vanguard and again in the approach of Jean II's *bataille* was entirely pedestrian; their numbers were not sufficient to overawe or suppress their English opponents, and their method of employment showed no particular imagination.

The reasoning must have been in part an expectation that the heavy cavalry of the Marshals would perform its role and scatter the English formations of archers, riding them down before they could take a toll on the advancing men-at-arms. Certainly the employment of heavily armoured knights and horses blunted the English archery of the Earl of Warwick's division to some degree, but only until a simple repositioning was effected. The adaptive tactics of the English archers in comparison, shown by their flexibility in manoeuvring to counter Marshal d'Audrehem's horse, their consistent assaults on the flanks of the formations of French men-at-arms, their employment (as part of a mixed retinue) in the Captal de Buch's surprise attack, and even in their adoption of the role of light foot troops when their arrows were exhausted, proved their value.

For France the capture of the king, the shame of the duc d'Orléans' behaviour, as well as the deaths of nearly 2,500 noble men-at-arms (with 1,900 more taken prisoner) was, as the *Chronique des quatre premiers Valois* notes, 'a great harm, a great pity, and damage irreparable' (quoted in Rogers 2000: 384). The loss was a catastrophic blow to the economy, martial power and self-esteem of the ruling classes of France, including the king. Civil strife and decades of disorder in the form of the Jacquerie and the rise of the free companies were the consequences of the crown's inability to defend or even police its own lands.

# Aftermath

Under the stewardship of Edward III, the English crown enjoyed over two decades of ascendancy over France that, given the generally poor reputation of English arms on the continent (and the increasingly parlous state of her possessions in Aquitaine for over 40 years prior to the outbreak of hostilities in 1337), was shocking, particularly to the French.

An image of the English army on the move underneath the banner of St George. By 1360 the consistent feats of English arms had ridden roughshod over the existing French military system, but such salad days were not to last. With a move towards positional warfare and refusing battle, the French blunted many of the English tactical advantages. (© The British Library Board, Royal 20 C VII f. 186)

The outbreak of Jacquerie, from the *Chroniques de France ou de St Denis*. Named for the popular peasant uprising in 1358, 'Jacquerie' became a term describing outbreaks of lawlessness and was a direct result of French failures in the war. The chronicler Jean le Bel describes the scene: 'It's now become clear the kingdom had been – as it still is – so battered and crushed in every region that none of its princes, barons and lords had the courage to oppose those men of low estate, thronging together from every country, who had spread across the kingdom of France to burn, destroy and pillage. These bands of men, termed robbers and pillagers, had supreme captains in charge of them in all parts of the realm, so powerful that all the people of the kingdom obeyed their rule' (Bryant 2015: 242). (© The British Library Board, Royal 20 C VII f. 133)

In the English armies of the period, 'as campaign followed campaign and armies were raised and disbanded, clusters of knights and sergeants rode together repeatedly and regularly serving captains were able to field retinues that were, in part at least, settled in composition' (Ayton 2011: 18). The English development of new models of recruitment, increased professionalization and tactical innovation 'was a "quiet revolution", involving institutional evolution, gradual development with occasional bursts of rapid change, frequently as much a consequence of the interplay of circumstances as of royal planning' (Ayton 1994: 36). The increasing numbers of mounted archers, as well as mixed retinues that contained both mounted archers and men-at-arms, meant that by 1360 English armies were of a fundamentally different character to those that had fought and lost so badly at Bannockburn 46 years before (Ayton 1994: 31–32).

The French armies, once the example to which all of Europe looked, were as much trapped by a romantic and at times wilfully unrealistic ethos of war as they were by outdated tactics. Some of the blame undoubtedly falls on the kings, Philippe VI and Jean II, neither of whom were made for battle, but the system of medieval kingship and control within which they exercised their power put tremendous weight on the shoulders of the monarch, amplifying both successes and mistakes in equal part. The French did understand, however haltingly at first, that they needed to change, and in the decades that succeeded the Treaty of Brétigny the reforms made to the army by Charles V in concert with the deployment of new strategies based on positional warfare would bring cold lessons to the English.

# BIBLIOGRAPHY

## Medieval sources

**Adam of Murimuth** (1274/75–1347) wrote the *Continuatio chronicarum*, covering the period from 1303 to 1347, its value coming from his extensive diplomatic experience. He was well acquainted with the political intricacies of Edwards III's claims against the French crown, having been involved in some of the negotiations himself, and supported his master's position, though he shows disappointment in the way that the war was conducted.

The ***Anonimalle Chronicle*** is an anonymous manuscript from several hands, composed at St Mary's Abbey, York, covering the years 1307–81. The first portion (dealing with events up to 1356) was probably written before 1382, and certain sections appear to have been copied wholesale from other sources. Clifford Rogers notes that the portion dealing with the Poitiers campaign 'was probably composed two or three decades later, but seems to have been based on eye-witness testimony' (Rogers 1999: 164).

The **Chandos Herald** (*fl.*1360s–80s) wrote a poem ('The Life and Deeds of the Black Prince', probably composed *c.*1376–87) extolling the virtues of Edward the Black Prince and his great friend (and the herald's master) John Chandos, who was killed in battle in 1369 at the age of 55. His value lies in his closeness to Chandos, one of the foremost knights of the time who played a significant role at both Crécy and Poitiers.

The ***French Chronicle of London***, covering the years 1259–1343, was composed by an anonymous author in the early years of the French war. The editor and translator H.T. Riley's description of this source is pithy and comprehensive: 'The "French Chronicle of London" is translated from the Norman French … we are justified in concluding that it was compiled in the earlier half of the 14th century; but by whom, or for what especial object, it is probably impossible to ascertain' (Riley 1863: xi).

The ***Grandes Chroniques de France***, a work of many hands over many years, was collated with ongoing incremental additions from the 13th to the 15th centuries. The chronicle – being a record of French history through the prism of French (and Frankish) royal families – was for an exclusive readership. Originating at the abbey of Saint-Denis near Paris, the monks of that institution became the historiographers of France and presumably had access to significant resources when composing updated editions of the work.

**Jean le Bel** (*c.*1290–1370) composed his *True Chronicles* at the request of Jean de Beaumont, Count of Soissons. Having campaigned with Edward III (of whom he was a great admirer) in the Scottish wars of the 1330s, Jean le Bel had first-hand knowledge of the warfare of his day, giving his chronicle greater authority than most. He also used accounts of eyewitnesses and participants to ensure the accuracy of the events he recorded.

**Jean Froissart** (*c.*1333–*c.*1405) began his *Chronicles* sometime in the 1370s, detailing the history of the Hundred Years' War from 1328 to 1400. Froissart was a man of his age and tended to be more concerned with great men and their deeds than the life of a run-of-the-mill soldier; his work drew on earlier sources (acknowledging his debt to Jean le Bel), especially concerning the first phases of the war. The historian Jonathan Sumption states that 'Froissart is particularly unreliable' (Sumption 1990: x).

**Geoffrey the Baker of Swinbrook** (*fl.*1326–58) wrote two chronicles, the structures of which owe much to Adam of Murimuth, 'but whereas the latter is laconic and circumspect, Baker is expansive and opinionated' (Haines 2004). Haines notes that on the war Baker is 'remarkably well informed, despite occasional confusion of dates and a penchant for anti-French gossip' (Haines 2004), with detailed accounts of Sluys, Crécy and Poitiers that demonstrate the level of access that he must have had to contemporary documents as well as to eyewitnesses.

**Henry Knighton** (d. *c.*1396) produced a history of England covering the years 959 to 1366 in his major work, the *Chronicon* (started in 1379). His chronicle on the early stages of the war relied largely upon Lancastrian sources, especially those that related to Henry of Grosmont (later 1st Duke of Lancaster) who was present at Sluys, campaigned in Aquitaine, and was at the siege of Calais.

Written anonymously, the ***Lanercost Chronicle*** was likely composed by a canon of Lanercost Priory in Cumbria. Mainly concerned with the history of Scotland and the north of England during 1201–1346, the chronicle is uneven and shows signs of having been drawn from many extant sources.

**Lord Northburgh** (*c.*1300–61) was a well-travelled diplomat and king's counsellor (appointed in 1346) who became bishop of London in 1354. As he accompanied Edward III on the Crécy expedition he was an eyewitness to much of the campaign, his letters giving contemporaneous updates of the events he witnessed or of which he knew.

**Robert of Avesbury** (d. 1359) wrote *De gestis mirabilibus regis Edwardi tertii*, primarily concerned with Edward III's campaigns in the early stages of the French war; Robert's wholehearted support for his beloved king colours his version of events, his work concluding with the aftermath of Poitiers in 1356.

**Sir Thomas Gray of Heton** (d. 1369), author of the *Scalacronica*, provides testimony of many of the conflicts that the English kings had with the Scots, as well as the early stages of the Hundred Years' War, notably Poitiers (most likely from conversation or correspondence with eyewitnesses) and the campaign of 1359–60 in which he was a participant.

**Thomas of Burton** (d. 1437), chronicler and abbot of Meaux in Yorkshire, wrote his *Chronica monasterii de Melsa* between *c*.1388 and 1402. Concerned primarily with the history of his own Cistercian abbey, he also writes about more general historical matters, sourcing his material mainly from his own abbey's library.

## Modern sources

Allmand, Christopher T., ed. (1973). *Society at War: The Experience of England and France during the Hundred Years War*. Edinburgh: Oliver & Boyd.

Ashley, W.J., ed. (1887). *Edward III and His Wars, 1327–1360*. London: Edward Nutt.

Autrand, Françoise (2005). 'The Battle of Crécy: A Hard Blow for the Monarchy of France', in Andrew Ayton & Philip Preston, *The Battle of Crécy, 1346*. Woodbridge: Boydell Press, pp. 273–86.

Ayton, Andrew (1994). 'English Armies in the Fourteenth Century', in Anne Curry & Michael Hughes, eds, *Arms, Armies, and Fortifications in the Hundred Years War*. Woodbridge: Boydell Press, pp. 21–38.

Ayton, Andrew (1999). *Knights and Warhorses: Military Service and the English Aristocracy under Edward III*. Woodbridge: Boydell Press.

Ayton, Andrew (2005a). 'The Crécy Campaign', in Andrew Ayton & Philip Preston, *The Battle of Crécy, 1346*. Woodbridge: Boydell Press, pp. 35–108.

Ayton, Andrew (2005b). 'The English Army at Crécy', in Andrew Ayton & Philip Preston, *The Battle of Crécy, 1346*. Woodbridge: Boydell Press, pp. 159–252.

Ayton, Andrew (2011). 'Military Service and the Dynamics of Recruitment in Fourteenth-Century England', in Adrian R. Bell, Anne Curry, Adam Chapman, Andy King & David Simpkin, eds, *The Soldier Experience in the Fourteenth Century*. Woodbridge: Boydell Press: pp. 9–59.

Barber, Richard (1986). *The Life and Campaigns of the Black Prince: From Contemporary Letters, Diaries and Chronicles, Including Chandos Herald's 'Life of the Black Prince'*. Woodbridge: Boydell. (First published by the Folio Society, 1979.)

Bennett, Matthew (1994). 'The Development of Battle Tactics in the Hundred Years War', in Anne Curry & Michael Hughes, eds, *Arms, Armies, and Fortifications in the Hundred Years War*. Woodbridge: Boydell Press, pp. 1–20.

Bourke, Paul & Wetham, David (2015). 'A Report of the Findings of the Defence Academy Warbow Trials Part 1 Summer 2005', in *Arms & Armour* 4.1: 53–81.

Bradbury, Jim (1997). *The Medieval Archer*. Woodbridge: Boydell Press. (First published 1985.)

Brereton, Geoffrey, trans., ed. (1978) *Froissart. Chronicles*. London: Penguin.

Bryant, Nigel, trans. (2015). *The True Chronicles of Jean le Bel, 1290–1360*. Woodbridge: Boydell Press.

Curry, Anne (2002). *The Hundred Years' War 1337–1453*. Essential Histories 19. Oxford: Osprey Publishing.

Cushway, Graham (2011). *Edward III and the War at Sea: The English Navy, 1327–1377*. Woodbridge: Boydell Press.

DeVries, Kelly (1995). 'God, Leadership, Flemings and Archery. Contemporary Perspectives of Victory and Defeat at the Battle of Sluys, 1340', in *American Neptune*, Vol. 55: 223–42. Available online at: http://deremilitari.org/wp-content/uploads/2014/03/devries2.pdf (accessed 1 April 2016).

DeVries, Kelly (1996). *Infantry Warfare in the Early Fourteenth Century: Discipline, Tactics, and Technology*. Woodbridge: Boydell Press.

DeVries, Kelly (2007). 'The Introduction and Use of the Pavise in the Hundred Years War', in *Arms & Armour*, 4.2: 93–100. Available online at: http://dx.doi.org/10.1179/174962607X229834 (accessed 9 August 2016).

DeVries, Kelly (2008). 'Medieval Mercenaries: Methodology, Definitions and Problems', in John France, ed., *Mercenaries and Paid Men: The Mercenary Identity in the Middle Ages*. Leiden: Brill, pp. 43–60.

DeVries, Kelly (2011). 'The Question of Medieval Military Professionalism', in Michael S. Neiberg, ed., *Arms and the Man: Military History Essays in Honor of Dennis Showalter*. Leiden: Brill, pp. 113–30.

Gribit, Nicholas A. (2016). *Henry of Lancaster's Expedition to Aquitaine, 1345–46: Military Service and Professionalism in the Hundred Years War*. Woodbridge: Boydell.

Haines, Roy Martin (2004). 'Baker, Geoffrey le (fl. 1326–1358)', in *Oxford Dictionary of National Biography*. Oxford: Oxford University Press. Found online at: http://www.oxforddnb.com/view/article/1114 (accessed 8 May 2016).

Hardy, Robert (1998). 'The Military Archery at Neville's Cross, 1346', in David Rollason & Michael Prestwich, eds, *The Battle of Neville's Cross 1346*. Donington: Shaun Tyas, pp. 112–31.

Available online at: http://web.archive.org/web/20101229173444/http://www.deremilitari.org/resources/pdfs/hardy.pdf (accessed 8 May 2016).

Jones, Robert W. (2010). *Bloodied Banners: Martial Display on the Medieval Battlefield*. Woodbridge: Boydell Press.

Lambert, Craig L. (2011). *Shipping the Medieval Military: English Maritime Logistics in the Fourteenth Century*. Woodbridge: Boydell Press.

Livingstone, Marilyn & Witzel, Morgen (2005). *The Road to Crécy: The English Invasion of France, 1346*. Harlow: Pearson.

Martin, G.H., trans., ed. (1995). *Knighton's Chronicle 1337–1396*. Oxford Medieval Texts. Oxford: Oxford University Press.

Maxwell, Sir Herbert Eustace, trans. & ed. (1913). *The Chronicle of Lanercost, 1272–1346*. Glasgow: James Maclehose & Sons.

Nicolle, David (2000). *French Armies of the Hundred Years War*. Men-at-Arms 337. Oxford: Osprey Publishing.

Nicolle, David (2004). *Poitiers 1356: The Capture of a King*. Campaign 138. Oxford: Osprey Publishing.

Nicolle, David (2011). *European Medieval Tactics (1): The Fall and Rise of Cavalry 450–1260*. Elite 185. Oxford: Osprey Publishing.

Nicolle, David (2012). *European Medieval Tactics (2): New Infantry, New Weapons 1260–1500*. Elite 189. Oxford: Osprey Publishing.

Preest, David, trans., & Barber, Richard (2012). *The Chronicle of Geoffrey le Baker*. Woodbridge: Boydell Press.

Preston, Sir Philip (2005). 'The Traditional Battlefield of Crécy', in Andrew Ayton & Philip Preston, *The Battle of Crécy, 1346*. Woodbridge: Boydell Press, pp. 109–38.

Prestwich, Michael (2005). 'The Battle of Crécy', in Andrew Ayton & Philip Preston, *The Battle of Crécy, 1346*. Woodbridge: Boydell Press, pp. 139–58.

Riley, Henry Thomas, trans. & ed. (1863). *Chronicles of the Mayors and Sheriffs of London A.D. 1188 to A.D. 1274; The French Chronicle of London A.D. 1259 to A.D. 1343*. London: Trübner & Co.

Rogers, Clifford. J. (1993). 'The Military Revolutions of the Hundred Years' War', in *The Journal of Military History*, 57.2: 241–78. Available online at http://deremilitari.org/2014/06/the-military-revolutions-of-the-hundred-years-war/ (accessed 1 April 2016).

Rogers, Clifford. J., ed. (1999). *The Wars of Edward III: Sources and Interpretations*. Woodbridge: Boydell Press.

Rogers, Clifford. J. (2000). *War Cruel and Sharp: English Strategy under Edward III, 1327–1360*. Woodbridge: Boydell Press.

Schnerb, Bertrand (2005). 'Vassals, Allies and Mercenaries: the French Army before and after 1346', in Andrew Ayton & Philip Preston, *The Battle of Crécy, 1346*. Woodbridge: Boydell Press, pp. 265-72.

Strickland, Matthew & Hardy, Robert (2005). *The Great Warbow: From Hastings to the Mary Rose*. Stroud: Sutton Publishing.

Sumption, Jonathan (1990). *The Hundred Years War, Volume 1: Trial by Battle*. London: Faber & Faber.

Sumption, Jonathan (1999). *The Hundred Years War, Volume 2: Trial by Fire*. London: Faber & Faber.

Thompson, Edward Maunde, ed. (1889). *Chronicon Galfridi le Baker de Swynebroke*. Oxford: Clarendon Press.

Vale, Malcolm (1994). 'The War in Aquitaine', in Anne Curry & Michael Hughes, eds, *Arms, Armies, and Fortifications in the Hundred Years War*. Woodbridge: Boydell Press, pp. 69–82.

Wadge, Richard (2013). *Arrowstorm: The World of the Archer In The Hundred Years War*. Stroud: The History Press. (First published 2009.)

Waller, Jonathan & Waller, John (2015). 'The Personal Carriage of Arrows from Hastings to the Mary Rose', in *Arms & Armour*, 7.2: 155–77.

An image of devils roaming the land from the Queen Mary Psalter. The accepted method of making war through the *chevauchée* wasn't always seen as honourable or justified, as demonstrated by a quote from the poet Eustache Deschamps in 1369: 'Soldiers destroy the country through pillage, all honour is gone, they like to be called gens d'armes but they roam the country, destroying everything in their way, and the poor people are forced to flee before them. If the soldier manages to travel three leagues in a day he thinks he has done well' (Nicolle 2000: 6). (© The British Library Board, Royal 2 B VII f. 213v)

# INDEX

80